THE HOLISTIC LEARNING HANDBOOK

MIND

SPIRIT

HEART

BODY

A PRACTICAL GUIDE FOR TEACHERS, TRAINERS AND FACILITATORS OF LEARNING

BY NICKI DAVEY AND LAUREN GOODEY

Matador
9 Priory Business Park,
Wistow Road, Kibworth Beauchamp,
Leicestershire. LE8 0RX
Tel: 0116 279 2299
Email: books@troubador.co.uk
Web: www.troubador.co.uk/matador
Twitter: @matadorbooks

ISBN 978 1800460 904

British Library Cataloguing in Publication Data.
A catalogue record for this book is available from the British Library.

Printed and bound by CPI Group (UK) Ltd, Croydon, CR0 4YY

Matador is an imprint of Troubador Publishing Ltd

CONTENTS

WELCOME TO THE HOLISTIC LEARNING HANDBOOK

WELCOME TO THE HOLISTIC LEARNING HANDBOOK

IF YOU'RE A TRAINER, TEACHER OR EDUCATOR OF ANY KIND WHOSE ROLE IS TO HELP OTHERS LEARN, AND YOU'RE LOOKING FOR PRACTICAL IDEAS TO MAKE YOUR TRAINING OR TEACHING MORE ENGAGING, EFFECTIVE OR MEANINGFUL...

THIS BOOK IS FOR YOU!

WHAT MAKES IT A HOLISTIC LEARNING HANDBOOK?

THIS BOOK IS BASED ON THE FUNDAMENTAL PRINCIPLE THAT DEEP, MEANINGFUL LEARNING WHICH ACTUALLY CHANGES BEHAVIOUR NEEDS TO BE HOLISTIC, I.E. IT HAPPENS ON A PHYSICAL, INTELLECTUAL, EMOTIONAL AND SPIRITUAL LEVEL. THE BODY, MIND, HEART AND SPIRIT ARE ALL INTERCONNECTED AND LEARNING SHOULD THEREFORE INVOLVE MULTIPLE LAYERS OF STIMULUS, MEANING AND EXPERIENCE TO ENGAGE THE WHOLE PERSON. THIS WILL THEN CREATE THE DEEP UNDERSTANDING WHICH LEADS TO BEHAVIOURAL CHANGE.

A HANDBOOK IS A CONCISE MANUAL WHICH GIVES SPECIFIC INSTRUCTIONS AND CAN BE USED AS A READY REFERENCE. THIS HANDBOOK CONSISTS OF EASILY DIGESTIBLE CHUNKS OF PRACTICAL INFORMATION AND OFFERS TIPS, IDEAS, INSPIRATION AND ADVICE ON HOW TO MAKE LEARNING HOLISTIC BY ENGAGING THE BODY, THE MIND, THE HEART AND THE SPIRIT OF LEARNERS.

WHY IS IT ILLUSTRATED?

AN IMPORTANT AND WELL-ESTABLISHED FACT IS THAT WHEN IT COMES TO LEARNING, VISION IS THE MOST INFLUENTIAL OF THE SENSES. SINCE INFORMATION CAN BE TRANSFERRED MORE QUICKLY AND MORE EFFECTIVELY IN PICTURES THAN IN WORDS, THE CONTENT HAS BEEN BROUGHT TO LIFE WITH ILLUSTRATION, MAKING IT BOTH EASY TO USE AND ENJOYABLE TO LOOK AT. EACH SECTION IS COLOUR CODED TO HELP YOU ANCHOR THE INFORMATION AND IDEAS OUTLINED IN EACH CHAPTER

HOW TO USE THIS BOOK

WE'VE DESIGNED THIS BOOK SO THAT YOU CAN READ IT FROM COVER TO COVER  OR DIP INTO IT FOR REFERENCE AND RETURN TIME AND TIME AGAIN FOR NEW IDEAS AND INSPIRATION.

THE BOOK HAS FOUR SECTIONS

EACH SECTION HAS THREE CHAPTERS

BODY

MIND

HEART

SPIRIT

NEUROSCIENCE AND BEHAVIOURAL PSYCHOLOGY HAVE TRANSFORMED OUR UNDERSTANDING OF HOW THE BRAIN WORKS AND HOW PEOPLE LEARN, AND THIS BOOK IS DESIGNED TO TRANSLATE SOME OF THE KEY FINDINGS FROM THE LATEST SCIENCE INTO SIMPLE, AFFORDABLE, PRACTICAL IDEAS THAT YOU CAN USE WHEN TEACHING OR TRAINING OTHERS. WE'VE ALSO INCLUDED LOTS OF TRIED AND TESTED TECHNIQUES AND APPROACHES WHICH HAVE EMERGED FROM MANY YEARS OF TRAINING EXPERIENCE COMBINED WITH AN INTUITIVE SENSE OF WHAT REALLY WORKS.

SO WHATEVER YOU'RE HELPING PEOPLE TO LEARN, AND HOWEVER YOU ARE DOING IT, WE HOPE YOU WILL FIND THIS BOOK USEFUL, INFORMATIVE AND INSPIRING. WE HOPE YOU WILL BRING YOUR BODY, MIND, HEART + SPIRIT TO IT - WHETHER IT'S BY SCRIBBLING IN THE MARGINS, COLOURING IN THE PICTURES, CARRYING OUT FURTHER RESEARCH, SHARING IT WITH YOUR COLLEAGUES OR PLAYING + EXPERIMENTING WITH THE IDEAS.

EACH CHAPTER HAS A BRIEF EXPLANATION OF THE REASONING AND THE SCIENCE BEHIND THE PARTICULAR PRINCIPLE WHICH IT ADVOCATES, AND IS PACKED FULL OF PRACTICAL ADVICE AND IDEAS FOR PUTTING THIS PRINCIPLE INTO PRACTICE.

MOST OF ALL WE HOPE YOU HAVE FUN WITH IT, AND WE WARMLY INVITE YOU TO JOIN US ON THE PATH TO HOLISTIC LEARNING.

Part one

HOW TO CREATE A POSITIVE PHYSICAL STATE FOR LEARNING

WHEN OUR BODY IS IN A RELAXED BUT ALERT STATE, OUR MIND PROCESSES INFORMATION AND IDEAS BETTER AND CREATES STRONGER MEMORIES, LEADING TO BETTER LEARNING.

THE BODY AND MIND ARE INEXTRICABLY CONNECTED ON BOTH A PHYSICAL AND CHEMICAL LEVEL. MESSENGERS SUCH AS HORMONES AND NEUROTRANSMITTERS PROVIDE A CONSTANT COMMUNICATION BETWEEN THE MIND AND BODY SO THAT OUR MENTAL STATE AFFECTS THE BODY'S BIOLOGICAL FUNCTIONING, AND OUR PHYSICAL STATE AFFECTS OUR MENTAL + COGNITIVE FUNCTIONING.

BODY

AS FACILITATORS OF LEARNING WE SHOULD PAY ATTENTION TO THESE CONNECTIONS AND CREATE AN ENVIRONMENT WITHIN THE BODY THAT ENABLES THE BRAIN TO LEARN.

SOME FACTORS THAT CONTRIBUTE TO A POSITIVE PHYSICAL LEARNING STATE MAY BE OUTSIDE OUR CONTROL (SUCH AS HOW MUCH SLEEP LEARNERS HAVE HAD), HOWEVER WE CAN TAKE STEPS TO MAKE SURE LEARNERS UNDERSTAND THE IMPACT OF THESE FACTORS ON THEIR ABILITY TO LEARN, AND ENCOURAGE THEM TO TAKE MORE RESPONSIBILITY FOR THEMSELVES + THEIR OWN LEARNING STATE.

WE CAN ALSO DO A LOT TO HELP LEARNERS GET INTO A PHYSICAL STATE THAT IS CONDUCIVE TO LEARNING. HERE ARE SOME KEY FACTORS TO PAY ATTENTION TO, ALONG WITH TIPS FOR PUTTING THEM INTO PRACTICE...

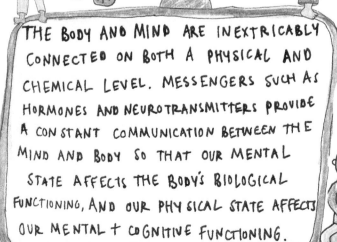

SUFFICIENT GOOD QUALITY SLEEP IS CRITICAL FOR LEARNING & MEMORY.

SLEEP ZZZ

USE PRE-COURSE INFORMATION TO ENCOURAGE LEARNERS TO GET A GOOD NIGHT'S SLEEP BEFORE THE TRAINING AS IT WILL HELP THEM LEARN BETTER

RECCOMMEND THAT LEARNERS AVOID CAFFEINE IN THE LATE AFTERNOON & EVENING AND STOP USING SCREENS, WHICH SUPPRESS THE PRODUCTION OF SLEEP-INDUCING HORMONE MELATONIN, AT LEAST AN HOUR BEFORE BED.

ENCOURAGE LEARNERS TO ENSURE THAT THEY GET A GOOD NIGHT'S SLEEP AFTER THE TRAINING SO THAT THE MEMORIES CAN BE CONSOLIDATED EFFECTIVELY

CREATE TRAINING ACTIVITIES OR GAMES WHICH INCORPORATE THE DRINKING OF WATER

BRAIN HYDRATION

PROVIDE WATER AND REMIND LEARNERS TO SIP REGULARLY

AVOID SALTY SNACKS OR MEALS WHICH DEHYDRATE THE BRAIN

A HYDRATED BRAIN IS ESSENTIAL FOR PROCESSING INFORMATION, CREATING MEMORIES AND MAINTAINING ATTENTION & CONCENTRATION

CHOOSE A ROOM OR VENUE WITH COMFORTABLE, MOVEABLE CHAIRS.

MAKE SURE LEARNERS KNOW WHEN BREAKS AND MEALS WILL TAKE PLACE SO THAT THEY CAN MANAGE THEIR OWN COMFORT.

BODY

Hi

INTRODUCE YOURSELF WITH A FRIENDLY, INFORMAL HELLO

PROVIDE INFORMATION ABOUT THE FACILITATORS SO LEARNERS FEEL THEY KNOW THE PERSON

PHYSICAL COMFORT

BUILD IN UNPLANNED COMFORT BREAKS IF LEARNERS' BODY LANGUAGE SUGGESTS THEY ARE UNCOMFORTABLE

OUTLINE WHAT LEARNERS WILL LEARN AND THE SORTS OF ACTIVITIES THEY'LL BE DOING.

PRE-COURSE PREPARATION

CHECK IN WITH LEARNERS AND ENCOURAGE THEM TO TELL YOU IF THEY ARE HOT/COLD/HUNGRY /UNCOMFORTABLE AND ADJUST ACCORDINGLY.

ENCOURAGE LEARNERS TO WEAR CLOTHES THAT THEY FEEL COMFORTABLE AND RELAXED IN, AND TO WEAR LAYERS FOR EASY TEMPERATURE REGULATION

PROVIDE USEFUL INFORMATION SUCH AS WHAT MATERIALS TO BRING, ADVICE ON WHY THEY NEED A GOOD NIGHTS SLEEP, WHAT TO WEAR ETC.

GIVE ENOUGH INFORMATION ABOUT LOCATION, VENUE, TRAVEL, PARKING ETC FOR LEARNERS TO PLAN THEIR JOURNEY AND ARRIVE UNFLUSTERED

CHOOSE VENUES/ROOMS WITH DÉCOR THAT IS GOOD FOR LEARNING: PALE, MUTED COLOURS FOR CALMNESS WITH SPLASHES OF BRIGHTER COLOURS TO PROVIDE VISUAL STIMULATION TO MAKE LEARNERS FEEL RELAXED YET ALERT, CALM YET STIMULATED.

CREATE AN ENVIRONMENT WHICH STIMULATES THE SENSES WITH COLOURS, IMAGES, TEXTURES, SOUNDS, SMELLS AND TASTES (SEE CHAPTER 1.2 HOW TO ENGAGE ALL THE SENSES

REARRANGE FURNITURE TO MAKE THE ROOM FEEL MORE INTIMATE. TAKE AWAY ANY UNNECESSARY BARRIERS SUCH AS TABLES, AND BRING LEARNERS CLOSE TO YOU AND EACH OTHER

PHYSICAL ENVIRONMENT

USE SOFT LIGHTING TO CREATE A CALM STATE - BRING YOUR OWN LAMPS OR CANDLES IF NECESSARY.

BODY

AVOID VENUES OR ROOMS WITH FLUORESCENT LIGHTING WHICH TRIGGERS THE STRESS HORMONE CORTISOL AND INHIBITS LEARNING.

MAXIMISE NATURAL LIGHT TO INCREASE ATTENTION, ALERTNESS, MEMORY AND RECALL - CHOOSE ROOMS WITH WINDOWS AND OPEN ALL THE BLINDS & CURTAINS

USE A VENUE WITH FURNITURE & FITTINGS MADE FROM NATURAL MATERIALS WHICH ARE SHOWN TO MAKE PEOPLE FEEL MORE EMOTIONALLY POSITIVE.

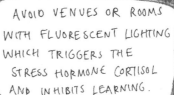

FRUITS
GRAPES
POMEGRANATES
ORANGES
BANANAS

OILY FISH
SALMON
TUNA
MACKEREL
SARDINES

SEEDS
PUMPKIN
SUNFLOWER
FLAX
SESAME

WHOLE GRAINS
BROWN RICE
OATS

AVOID FOODS THAT INHIBIT LEARNING, SUCH AS:
• REFINED WHEAT PRODUCTS (WHITE BREAD, PASTRIES, CAKES)
• SUGAR (CAKES, BISCUITS, DESSERTS)
• SATURATED FATS + FRIED FOODS
• ARTIFICIAL FOOD ADDITIVES (SWEETENERS, FLAVOURING, COLOURING + PRESERVATIVES)

BODY

NUTS + NUT BUTTERS
ALMONDS
WALNUTS
CASHEWS
HAZELS
BRAZILS
PEANUTS

PROVIDE HEALTHY SNACKS + NIBBLES SUCH AS NUTS, SEEDS, DRIED FRUIT, FRESH FRUIT + SMALL AMOUNTS OF DARK CHOCOLATE TO MAINTAIN BLOOD SUGAR LEVELS, STIMULATE TASTE BUDS, TO IMPROVE ATTENTION + ALERTNESS + WARD OFF HUNGER PANGS

USE RELAXING ESSENTIAL OILS IN AN OIL BURNER SUCH AS LAVENDER, ROSE OR BERGAMOT

BERRIES
BLUEBERRIES
STRAWBERRIES

BEANS LENTILS & PULSES

BRAIN FRIENDLY FOOD

PLAY RELAXING MUSIC

RELAXATION

PROVIDE FOOD THAT IS GOOD FOR THE BRAIN, AND BOOSTS CONCENTRATION, ALERTNESS, BRAIN FUNCTION + MEMORY:

HERBAL TEAS THAT ARE DESIGNED TO BOOST ALERTNESS

LEAFY GREENS SUCH AS SPINACH KALE CABBAGE

CONNECT LEARNERS WITH NATURE, WHICH IS PROVEN TO RELAX PEOPLE.
SEE CHAPTER 4.2 HOW TO USE NATURE TO HELP PEOPLE LEARN

USE MEDITATIVE, REPETITIVE ACTIVITIES THAT RELAX PEOPLE SUCH AS COLOURING OR WALKING OUTDOORS

DARK CHOCOLATE  **AVOCADOS**

BRIGHTLY COLOURED VEG
CARROTS
RED PEPPERS

IF LEARNERS BRING THEIR OWN MEALS, ENCOURAGE THEM TO BRING LIGHT MEALS BASED ON FRESH FRUIT, VEG, WHOLEGRAINS + FISH.

USE SIMPLE RELAXATION TECHNIQUES TO CREATE A RELAXED LEARNING STATE (SEE APPENDIX 1 FOR EXAMPLES OF EASY BUT EFFECTIVE TECHNIQUES)

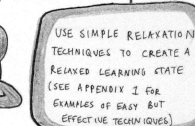

BODY

HOW TO ENGAGE ALL THE SENSES

THE SENSORY ORGANS ARE "THE WINDOW TO THE BRAIN".

THE MORE SENSORY STIMULATION WE RECEIVE, THE MORE NEURAL CONNECTIONS ARE MADE. THIS IMPROVES THE ORGANISATION AND FUNCTIONAL ACTIVITY OF OUR BRAIN.

STIMULATING ALL THE SENSES HELPS LEARNERS TO FORM LONG LASTING MEMORIES AND TO EMBED THE LEARNING SO THAT THEY RECALL AND USE WHAT THEY LEARNT VERY QUICKLY AND EASILY.

DON'T USE SENSORY ACTIVITIES AS AN ADD ON OR A GIMMICK JUST TO MAKE TRAINING MORE INTERESTING OR FUN.

USE SENSORY ACTIVITIES AS AN INTEGRAL PART OF THE LEARNING PROCESS.

USE VISUALS, TEXTURES, SOUNDS, TASTES AND SMELLS TO:

 INFLUENCE THE MOOD OF THE LEARNERS OR CREATE A PARTICULAR STATE (EG RELAXED, CALM, CREATIVE, ENERGISED)

 INCREASE LEARNERS' CONCENTRATION AND KEEP THEM ALERT

 MAKE LEARNERS' MORE AWARE OF THEIR SURROUNDINGS AND EXPERIENCES

 ANCHOR LEARNING BY ASSOCIATING DIFFERENT SMELLS, SIGHTS, TASTES, SOUNDS, TOUCH SENSATIONS OR MOVEMENTS WITH DIFFERENT FACTS OR LEARNING POINTS

 HELP LEARNERS UNDERSTAND BY USING SENSORY ACTIVITIES TO ILLUSTRATE OR EXPLORE A TOPIC OR LEARNING POINT

 IMPROVE MEMORY AND RECALL BY USING MORE AREAS OF THE BRAIN SIMULTANEOUSLY

RECREATE OR SIMULATE REAL SITUATIONS SO THAT LEARNERS CAN CONNECT THE LEARNING TO REAL LIFE EXPERIENCES

LEO

HERE ARE SOME SIMPLE THINGS YOU CAN DO...

TOUCH

Provide fiddle toys for people to handle and play with during the course

Ask learners to make their own name badges from craft materials

Give people course resources or materials in a gift box which they can handle + open / close

Use different physical actions or movements as anchors for different learning points

Ask learners to create playdoh models to show how they feel, who they are, what they've learnt etc.

Use games + activities that involve touching, holding + moving items

Ask learners to make a sculpture or collage to illustrate an idea or learning point

Give out magazines and scissors and ask learners to cut out images to represent key learning points

Provide different textured materials - ask learners to associate different meanings with these

Pass around a juggling ball to show whose turn it is to speak

BODY

Put pots of fresh herbs on tables and encourage learners to touch them to release the aromas

Put highly scented flowers such as stocks, roses or freesias in the room

Ask learners to choose a smell to associate with their learning or how they feel

SMELL

Use sprigs of fresh herbs to divide people into groups, encourage them to handle and smell these

Create a different ambience in each work space or break out room by using different scents

Use essential oils to create different moods

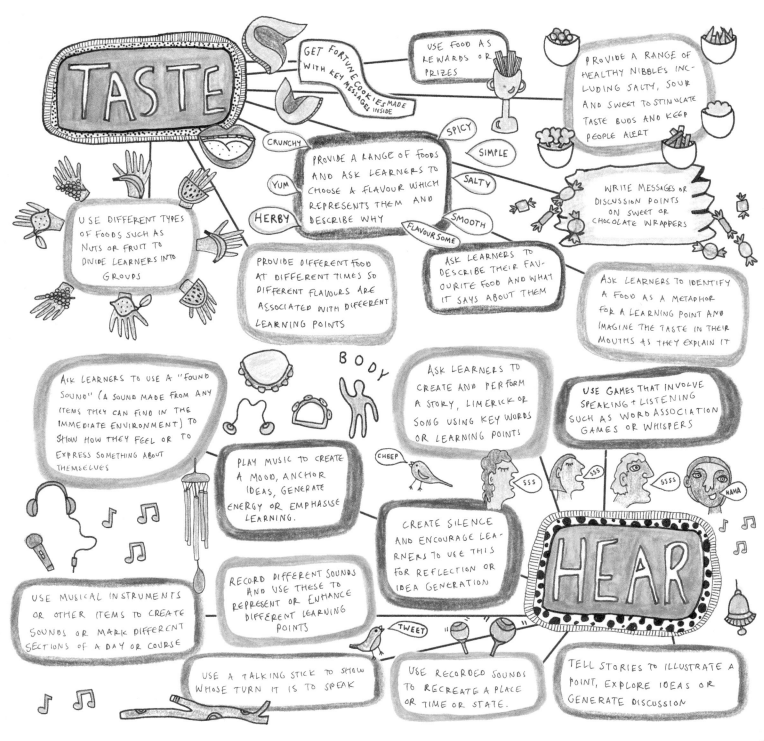

TASTE

GET FORTUNE COOKIES MADE WITH KEY MESSAGES INSIDE

USE FOOD AS REWARDS OR PRIZES

PROVIDE A RANGE OF HEALTHY NIBBLES INCLUDING SALTY, SOUR AND SWEET TO STIMULATE TASTE BUDS AND KEEP PEOPLE ALERT

SPICY

CRUNCHY

SIMPLE

YUM

PROVIDE A RANGE OF FOODS AND ASK LEARNERS TO CHOOSE A FLAVOUR WHICH REPRESENTS THEM AND DESCRIBE WHY

SALTY

HERBY

SMOOTH

FLAVOURSOME

WRITE MESSAGES OR DISCUSSION POINTS ON SWEET OR CHOCOLATE WRAPPERS

USE DIFFERENT TYPES OF FOODS SUCH AS NUTS OR FRUIT TO DIVIDE LEARNERS INTO GROUPS

PROVIDE DIFFERENT FOOD AT DIFFERENT TIMES SO DIFFERENT FLAVOURS ARE ASSOCIATED WITH DIFFERENT LEARNING POINTS

ASK LEARNERS TO DESCRIBE THEIR FAVOURITE FOOD AND WHAT IT SAYS ABOUT THEM

ASK LEARNERS TO IDENTIFY A FOOD AS A METAPHOR FOR A LEARNING POINT AND IMAGINE THE TASTE IN THEIR MOUTHS AS THEY EXPLAIN IT

ASK LEARNERS TO USE A "FOUND SOUND" (A SOUND MADE FROM ANY ITEMS THEY CAN FIND IN THE IMMEDIATE ENVIRONMENT) TO SHOW HOW THEY FEEL OR TO EXPRESS SOMETHING ABOUT THEMSELVES

BODY

ASK LEARNERS TO CREATE AND PERFORM A STORY, LIMERICK OR SONG USING KEY WORDS OR LEARNING POINTS

USE GAMES THAT INVOLVE SPEAKING + LISTENING SUCH AS WORD ASSOCIATION GAMES OR WHISPERS

PLAY MUSIC TO CREATE A MOOD, ANCHOR IDEAS, GENERATE ENERGY OR EMPHASISE LEARNING.

CHEEP

SSS

SSS

SSSS

HAHA

CREATE SILENCE AND ENCOURAGE LEARNERS TO USE THIS FOR REFLECTION OR IDEA GENERATION

HEAR

USE MUSICAL INSTRUMENTS OR OTHER ITEMS TO CREATE SOUNDS OR MARK DIFFERENT SECTIONS OF A DAY OR COURSE

RECORD DIFFERENT SOUNDS AND USE THESE TO REPRESENT OR ENHANCE DIFFERENT LEARNING POINTS

TWEET

USE A TALKING STICK TO SHOW WHOSE TURN IT IS TO SPEAK

USE RECORDED SOUNDS TO RECREATE A PLACE OR TIME OR STATE.

TELL STORIES TO ILLUSTRATE A POINT, EXPLORE IDEAS OR GENERATE DISCUSSION

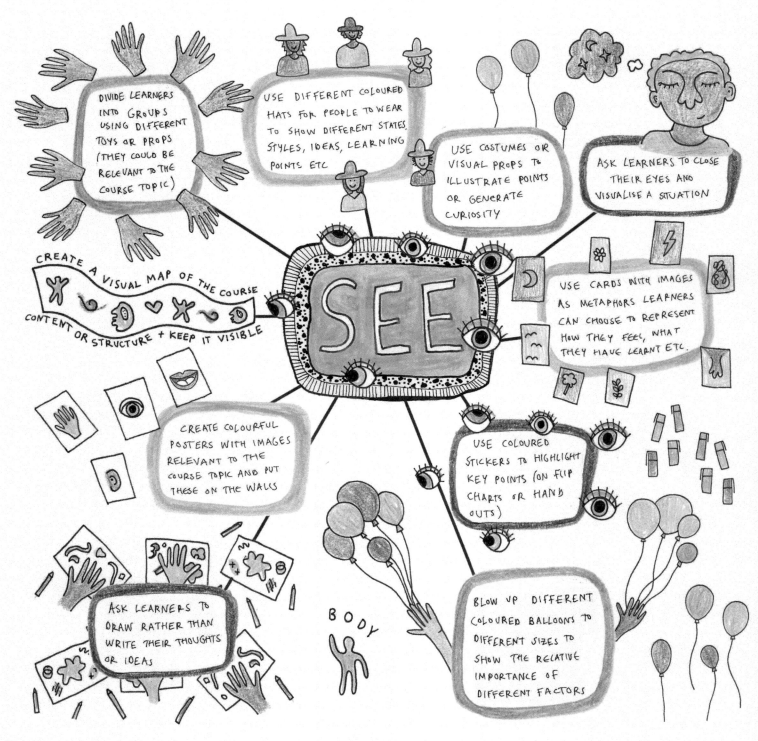

DIVIDE LEARNERS INTO GROUPS USING DIFFERENT TOYS OR PROPS (THEY COULD BE RELEVANT TO THE COURSE TOPIC)

USE DIFFERENT COLOURED HATS FOR PEOPLE TO WEAR TO SHOW DIFFERENT STATES, STYLES, IDEAS, LEARNING POINTS ETC

USE COSTUMES OR VISUAL PROPS TO ILLUSTRATE POINTS OR GENERATE CURIOSITY

ASK LEARNERS TO CLOSE THEIR EYES AND VISUALISE A SITUATION

CREATE A VISUAL MAP OF THE COURSE CONTENT OR STRUCTURE + KEEP IT VISIBLE

SEE

USE CARDS WITH IMAGES AS METAPHORS LEARNERS CAN CHOOSE TO REPRESENT HOW THEY FEEL, WHAT THEY HAVE LEARNT ETC.

CREATE COLOURFUL POSTERS WITH IMAGES RELEVANT TO THE COURSE TOPIC AND PUT THESE ON THE WALLS

USE COLOURED STICKERS TO HIGHLIGHT KEY POINTS (ON FLIP CHARTS OR HAND OUTS)

ASK LEARNERS TO DRAW RATHER THAN WRITE THEIR THOUGHTS OR IDEAS

BODY

BLOW UP DIFFERENT COLOURED BALLOONS TO DIFFERENT SIZES TO SHOW THE RELATIVE IMPORTANCE OF DIFFERENT FACTORS

HOW TO USE PHYSICAL MOVEMENT

BODY

HERE ARE SOME OF THE WAYS WHICH PHYSICAL ACTIVITY ENHANCES LEARNING:

MOVING AROUND HAS SIGNIFICANT EFFECTS ON OUR ABILITY TO LEARN, WITH STUDIES SHOWING THAT PHYSICAL MOVEMENT DURING OR IMMEDIATELY BEFORE LEARNING IMPROVES OUR COGNITIVE PROCESSING AND INCREASES OUR MEMORY + RECALL BY UP TO 20%.

AS FACILITATORS OF LEARNING, WE CAN CREATE OPPORTUNITIES AND ACTIVITIES WHICH ENCOURAGE AND ENABLE LEARNERS TO PHYSICALLY MOVE AROUND WHILST THEY ARE LEARNING. HERE ARE SOME TRIED + TESTED SUGGESTIONS FOR INCORPORATING MOVEMENT INTO LEARNING.

OXYGEN IS ESSENTIAL FOR GOOD BRAIN FUNCTION. PHYSICAL ACTIVITY INCREASES BLOOD FLOW AND THEREFORE OXYGEN LEVELS IN THE BRAIN - EVEN JUST STANDING UP INCREASES OXYGEN IN THE BRAIN BY 5-15%.

PHYSICAL ACTIVITY INCREASES THE BRAINS PRODUCTION OF BDNF (BRAIN-DERIVED NEUROTROPHIC FACTOR), WHICH IS ESSENTIAL FOR CREATING CONNECTIONS BETWEEN NEURONS, GENERATING NEW NEURONS, AND FORMING NEW NEURAL PATHWAYS. MOVING AROUND CREATES MORE, STRONGER NEURAL PATHWAYS AND THEREFORE LEADS TO DEEPER LEARNING.

THE CEREBELLUM (THE PART OF THE BRAIN THAT CO-ORDINATES PHYSICAL MOVEMENT + BALANCE) IS DIRECTLY LINKED TO THE PARTS OF THE BRAIN INVOLVED IN MEMORY, ATTENTION, AND SPACIAL PERCEPTION.

PHYSICAL EXCERCISE ACTIVATES THE CENTRAL NERVOUS SYSTEM AND STRENGTHENS THE AREAS OF THE BRAIN WHICH ARE USED FOR COGNITIVE PROCESSING, PROBLEM-SOLVING, CREATIVITY + MEMORY - ALL ESSENTIAL TO LEARNING.

PHYSICAL ACTIVITY IMPROVES MOOD AND BOOSTS THE MORALE AND MOTIVATION OF LEARNERS - THEY FEEL HAPPIER + MORE POSITIVE, WHICH IN TURN HELPS THEM TO LEARN BETTER.

USE DIFFERENT CORNERS OF THE ROOM TO REPRESENT DIFFERENT PARTS OF A CYCLE OR PROCESS + ASK LEARNERS TO STAND + MOVE BETWEEN THEM WHEN DISCUSSING / LEARNING ABOUT EACH STAGE

MIND BODY HEART SPIRIT

PUT POSTERS, IMAGES OR QUOTES RELEVANT TO THE TOPIC ON THE WALLS AND ASK LEARNERS TO WALK AROUND + READ THEM. ASK THEM TO STAND BY THE ONE THAT RESONATES MOST FOR THEM THEN INTRODUCE THEMSELVES AND EXPLAIN WHY THEY CHOSE IT.

BEGIN THE SESSION WITH A SIMPLE STRETCH, OR USE ENERGISING ACTIVITIES FROM YOGA OR QI GONG

SERVE LUNCHES & COFFEES IN A DIFFERENT ROOM FROM THE TRAINING TO ENCOURAGE MOVEMENT + PROVIDE DIFFERENT SENSORY STIMULI

BODY

USE PHYSICAL ANCHORING - LINK A PARTICULAR PHYSICAL MOVEMENT, GESTURE OR POSTURE TO A SPECIFIC LEARNING POINT SO THAT LEARNERS REMEMBER AND RECALL THE INFORMATION.

USE ROPES OR MASKING TAPE TO MAP OUT MODELS, PROCESSES OR GRAPHS...

AND ASK LEARNERS TO STAND AND MOVE AROUND ON THEM AS THEY EXPLORE OR DISCUSS THE KEY FEATURES OF EACH STAGE OR COMPONENT OF THE MODEL / PROCESS

PUT FLIPCHARTS FOR GROUP WORK ON THE WALL + ASK LEARNERS TO STAND UP TO DISCUSS OR WRITE THEIR IDEAS RATHER THAN WORKING AT TABLES

USE BALL THROWING GAMES TO REINFORCE OR REVIEW LEARNING

ASK LEARNERS TO WORK TOGETHER TO CREATE A SCULPTURE USING THEIR OWN BODIES AS A WAY TO ILLUSTRATE A SYSTEM OR REVIEW WHAT THEY HAVE LEARNT

INCORPORATE ACTIVITIES FROM DRAMA, MIME, DANCE ETC, EITHER AS ENERGISERS OR TO EXPLORE IDEAS, ILLUSTRATE POINTS OR REINFORCE LEARNING

part two

MIND

MIND

HOW TO USE PROBLEM SOLVING FOR LEARNING

WE LEARN BETTER IF WE LOOK FOR OR DISCOVER THE ANSWERS FOR OURSELVES RATHER THAN BEING GIVEN INFORMATION.

WHETHER WE'RE FIGURING OUT THE ANSWER TO A QUESTION, CONDUCTING AN EXPERIMENT TO SEE WHAT HAPPENS, OR FINDING THE SOLUTION TO A PUZZLE OR PROBLEM, WHEN WE WORK OUT THE ANSWER OURSELVES WE USE MORE PARTS OF OUR BRAIN, CREATING A "MENTAL WEB" OF INFORMATION ASSOCIATED WITH THE REQUIRED KNOWLEDGE OR SKILL. THIS HELPS US TO STORE, RETRIEVE, AND USE WHAT WE HAVE LEARNT MORE EFFECTIVELY.

FOR EXAMPLE, WHEN PEOPLE ARE ASKED A QUESTION AND THEY GUESS THE ANSWER, EVEN IF THEY GET IT WRONG, THEY ACTIVATE DIFFERENT AREAS OF THE BRAIN SO THAT WHEN THEY ARE GIVEN THE CORRECT ANSWER, THEY REMEMBER AND CAN RECALL IT BETTER.

MISTAKES ARE AN IMPORTANT PART OF THE PROCESS. WHEN PEOPLE MAKE MISTAKES, THEY CAN REFLECT ON THE RESULTS, RESPONSES, OR OUTCOMES, EXAMINE WHAT WENT WRONG, AND IDENTIFY ALTERNATIVE APPROACHES OR SOLUTIONS. THE TRAINING OR CLASSROOM PROVIDES A SAFE SPACE TO DO THIS, AND GETTING IT WRONG CAN LEAD TO MUCH MORE POWERFUL LEARNING THAN IF LEARNERS GET IT RIGHT IN THE FIRST PLACE.

WHEN WE ENABLE LEARNERS TO FIND THE ANSWERS THEMSELVES, WE HELP THEM TO TAKE RESPONSIBILITY FOR THEIR OWN LEARNING AND TO BE AN ACTIVE PARTICIPANT RATHER THAN A PASSIVE RECIPIENT OF INFORMATION. PROBLEM-SOLVING & SELF-DISCOVERED LEARNING ALSO HELPS LEARNERS TO DEVELOP OTHER IMPORTANT SKILLS SUCH AS CURIOSITY, COLLABORATION, COMMUNICATION, AND CREATIVITY, ALL OF WHICH HELPS THEM TO BE MORE EFFECTIVE LEARNERS.

MIND

PROMOTE A PROBLEM-SOLVING MINDSET

MAKE IT SAFE FOR LEARNERS TO GET IT WRONG

◇ EXPLAIN THAT WE LEARN BETTER WHEN WE GET IT WRONG THEN REFLECT AND REVIEW, THAN IF WE GET IT RIGHT THE FIRST TIME.

◇ BE POSITIVE + ENCOURAGE OTHER LEARNERS TO BE POSITIVE WHEN SOMEONE GETS SOMETHING WRONG OR MAKES A MISTAKE

BEGIN A TRAINING COURSE WITH A THOUGHT PROVOKING QUESTION OR PROMPT THAT ENCOURAGES LEARNERS TO EXPLORE THE TOPIC AND THE PARTICULAR CHALLENGES THAT THEY FACE IN RELATION TO IT

ENCOURAGE LEARNERS TO EXPERIMENT AND EXPLORE BY ASKING "WHAT IF...?"

WHAT IF?

GET LEARNERS INTO A RELAXED STATE SO THAT THE PROBLEM-SOLVING PART OF THE BRAIN CAN WORK EFFECTIVELY. (SEE CHAPTER 1.1 FOR TECHNIQUES TO CREATE A RELAXED LEARNING STATE.)

CREATE QUIZZES, CROSSWORDS, AND OTHER PUZZLES WITH SOLUTIONS THAT ARE RELEVANT TO THE TRAINING TOPIC

BUY GAMES, PUZZLES AND TOYS (CHARITY SHOPS ARE A GREAT SOURCE) AND USE THEM FOR TRAINING ACTIVITIES. IDEAS INCLUDE:
JIGSAWS
CONSTRUCTION TOYS
PLAYING GAMES
BOARD GAMES
LOGIC PUZZLES

CREATE EXPERIMENTS – GET DIFFERENT GROUPS TO CARRY OUT THE SAME TASK UNDER DIFFERENT CONDITIONS THEN COMPARE RESULTS AND IDENTIFY WHAT THE RESULTS TELL THEM.

CREATE PUZZLES SIMULATIONS AND EXPERIMENTS

```
LEARN
X
PLAY
L
O
RELAX
E
```

GIVE LEARNERS CRAFT MATERIALS OR HOUSEHOLD ITEMS TO CREATE A MODEL OF A PROCESS OR A THEORY + THEN TRY IT OUT

CREATE SIMULATIONS OF REAL SITUATIONS USING PROPS, TOOLS, MOVEMENT, VOICES AND ANYTHING ELSE THAT COMES TO HAND AND ASK LEARNERS TO WORK OUT WHAT IT TELLS THEM

GIVE LEARNERS OBJECTS TO REPRESENT THE DIFFERENT ASPECTS OF A PROBLEM OR CHALLENGE-USING TOOLS OR PHYSICAL OBJECTS SPARKS CREATIVITY + HELPS PEOPLE FIND NEW SOLUTIONS

PROMOTE "DO-IT-YOURSELF"

Ask people to guess the answer to a question, or solution to a problem before giving them the answer or solution

Put learners into groups and ask them to work together to explore a topic and discover what they can about it before sharing this with the group

Give learners a problem or a topic and ask them to research it and draw conclusions or generate theories themselves then present this to the group.

If someone asks a question which you don't know the answer to, ask them to go and find the answer themselves rather than offering to find out for them.

When someone asks a question, ask learners what they think is the answer before giving your own response.

Give learners a real life scenario and ask them to evaluate and compare the possible courses of actions + outcomes

WHAT WOULD HAPPEN IF

HOW DID THAT MAKE A DIFFERENCE

HOW COULD YOU DO THIS DIFFERENTLY

WHAT COULD YOU DO DIFFERENTLY NEXT TIME

Use questions which focus on positive outcomes and solutions to probe.

HOW COULD THIS BE EFFECTIVE

HOW CAN YOU USE THIS INFORMATION

WHERE ELSE MIGHT YOU SEE THIS

HOW DID YOU DO THAT

Help learners to work out for themselves what to do rather than giving advice.

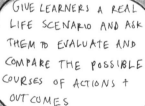

WHAT ARE THE BENEFITS OF THIS

Ask open questions such as "How could you use this information to...?" rather than closed questions such as "Could you use this information to help people to...?"

ASK GREAT QUESTIONS

WHY DO YOU THINK WE EXPLAIN IT LIKE THIS

WHY DO YOU THINK IT'S IMPORTANT TO UNDERSTAND THIS

WHAT DID YOU NOTICE WHEN YOU DID THIS

WHAT DO YOU THINK WORKS WELL

HOW TO ENGAGE DIFFERENT LEARNING AND THINKING STYLES

NEUROSCIENCE SUGGESTS THAT MANY LEARNING STYLE MODELS (SUCH AS THE VISUAL, AUDIO, KINAESTHETIC MODEL) ARE NO LONGER VALID, BUT WHAT IS CERTAIN IS THAT HOW WE LEARN IS AFFECTED BY MANY FACTORS SUCH AS INDIVIDUAL PREFERENCES, BRAIN DOMINANCES, PERSONAL PHYSIOLOGY, UPBRINGING, EDUCATIONAL BACKGROUND, CULTURAL NORMS, ETC. AS TRAINERS WE NEED TO RESPECT AND WORK WITH THIS DIVERSITY OF LEARNING, THINKING AND BEHAVIOURAL STYLES SO THAT EVERYONE CAN ENGAGE, WHATEVER THEIR PREFERENCES.

AS HUMAN BEINGS WE ALL DIFFER IN THE WAY WE THINK, COMMUNICATE AND BEHAVE. DIFFERENT PEOPLE ACROSS THE WORLD HAVE USED ARCHETYPES TO DESCRIBE DIFFERENT ASPECTS OF OUR PERSONALITIES, AND THOUSANDS OF YEARS LATER, PROFILING TOOLS AND OTHER MODELS ARE USED TO HELP PEOPLE UNDERSTAND DIFFERENT PERSONALITY TYPES. WE DIFFER IN HOW WE LIKE TO COMMUNICATE, HOW WE PROCESS INFORMATION, WHAT OUR PRIORITIES ARE, AND OUR PERSPECTIVE ON EVENTS AND SITUATIONS, WHICH HAS A DIRECT IMPACT ON HOW WE LEARN.

WE ARE ALL UNIQUE, AND THOSE OF US WHO HELP OTHER PEOPLE TO LEARN WILL KNOW FROM EXPERIENCE THAT DIFFERENT PEOPLE RESPOND BETTER TO SOME ACTIVITIES AND APPROACHES THAN TO OTHERS. FOR EXAMPLE, SOME PEOPLE LOVE TO EXPERIMENT AND TEST THINGS OUT AND ENJOY THE ELEMENT OF SURPRISE. FOR OTHERS THAT IS DEEPLY UNCOMFORTABLE, AND THEY PREFER TO OBSERVE AND REFLECT ON WHAT HAS HAPPENED TO MAKE SENSE OF THINGS. OUR NATURAL INCLINATION IS TO FACILITATE LEARNING IN A WAY THAT WE'D LIKE TO PARTICIPATE IN OURSELVES, AND THAT SUITS OUR OWN LEARNING STYLE, BUT WE MUST ALSO MEET THE NEEDS OF OTHER STYLES AND ENSURE THAT EVERY LEARNER CAN SUCCESSFULLY ENGAGE & LEARN.

HERE ARE SOME WAYS TO HELP ENSURE THAT YOU REACH AND ENGAGE DIVERSE LEARNING AND THINKING STYLES WHEN DESIGNING AND DELIVERING TRAINING.

DIFFERENT LEARNERS WILL PREFER TO WORK IN DIFFERENT WAYS OR FOCUS ON DIFFERENT STAGES OF THE LEARNING CYCLE:

MIND

HOW TO REWIRE THE BRAIN

THE HUMAN BRAIN CHANGES & DEVELOPS THROUGHOUT OUR LIVES IN RESPONSE TO DIFFERENT EXPERIENCES

THE BRAIN HAS BILLIONS OF NEURAL PATHWAYS THAT ARE ACTIVATED EVERYTIME WE DO SOMETHING, AND WHEN WE LEARN, THE NEURAL NETWORKS IN OUR BRAIN ARE MODIFIED. THE MORE A NETWORK OF NEURONS IS ACTIVATED, THE STRONGER THE CONNECTIONS BECOME. WHEN WE DO SOMETHING NEW OR THINK ABOUT SOMETHING DIFFERENTLY, A NEW NEURAL PATHWAY IS CREATED AND THE MORE WE DO OR THINK ABOUT THE SAME THING, THE MORE THAT PATHWAY IS REINFORCED AND BECOMES STRONGER. OTHER, UNUSED NEURAL PATHWAYS BECOME WEAKER AND DIE AWAY.

WHENEVER WE LEARN SOMETHING NEW IT REORGANISES ITSELF BY FORMING NEW CONNECTIONS (NEURAL PATHWAYS) BETWEEN DIFFERENT BRAIN CELLS (NEURONS). THE BRAIN NEVER STOPS CHANGING AS WE LEARN, AND THIS CAPACITY OF THE BRAIN TO CHANGE IS CALLED NEUROPLASTICITY.

IF PARTICULAR NEURONS KEEP FIRING AT THE SAME TIME, EVENTUALLY THEY DEVELOP A PHYSICAL CONNECTION.

"NEURONS THAT FIRE TOGETHER WIRE TOGETHER"

AS IF THEY ARE ELECTRICAL WIRES WRAPPED TOGETHER IN A BUNDLE AND WHEN ONE FIRES, THE OTHERS ARE TRIGGERED. THIS MEANS THAT OUR BRAIN LINKS DIFFERENT EXPERIENCES TOGETHER, FOR EXAMPLE IT MAY LINK A PARTICULAR EMOTION WITH A PARTICULAR SITUATION.

WHEN SOMEONE BECOMES AN EXPERT IN SOMETHING, THE AREAS OF THE BRAIN THAT DEAL WITH THIS SKILL OR KNOWLEDGE CHANGE OR GROW. FOR EXAMPLE, THE HIPPOCAMPUS (WHICH PROCESSES SPACIAL INFORMATION) OF LONDON TAXI DRIVERS IS LARGER + DENSER THAN THAT OF LONDON BUS DRIVERS, BECAUSE THEY DEVELOP A MENTAL MAP OF THE CITY (WHEREAS THE BUS DRIVERS DON'T AS THEY FOLLOW A FIXED ROUTE).

WE CAN EVEN CHANGE OUR BRAINS JUST BY IMAGINING DOING SOMETHING, BECAUSE THE BRAIN DOESN'T DISTINGUISH BETWEEN REAL OR IMAGINED ACTIVITY. BY VISUALISING DOING SOMETHING WE CAN CREATE THE SAME PHYSICAL CHANGES IN THE BRAIN AS IF WE WERE DOING IT FOR REAL.

WHEN WE FACILITATE LEARNING, WE'RE HELPING PEOPLE'S BRAINS TO CHANGE.

SO HERE ARE SOME SUGGESTIONS TO HELP WITH THIS...

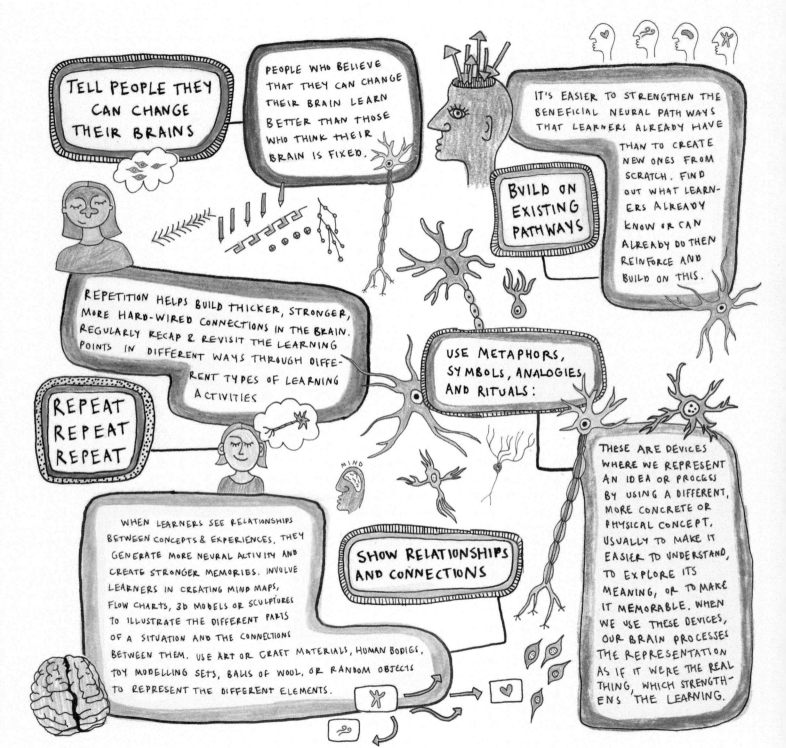

TELL PEOPLE THEY CAN CHANGE THEIR BRAINS

PEOPLE WHO BELIEVE THAT THEY CAN CHANGE THEIR BRAIN LEARN BETTER THAN THOSE WHO THINK THEIR BRAIN IS FIXED.

IT'S EASIER TO STRENGTHEN THE BENEFICIAL NEURAL PATHWAYS THAT LEARNERS ALREADY HAVE THAN TO CREATE NEW ONES FROM SCRATCH. FIND OUT WHAT LEARNERS ALREADY KNOW OR CAN ALREADY DO THEN REINFORCE AND BUILD ON THIS.

BUILD ON EXISTING PATHWAYS

REPETITION HELPS BUILD THICKER, STRONGER, MORE HARD-WIRED CONNECTIONS IN THE BRAIN. REGULARLY RECAP & REVISIT THE LEARNING POINTS IN DIFFERENT WAYS THROUGH DIFFERENT TYPES OF LEARNING ACTIVITIES

REPEAT REPEAT REPEAT

MIND

USE METAPHORS, SYMBOLS, ANALOGIES AND RITUALS:

WHEN LEARNERS SEE RELATIONSHIPS BETWEEN CONCEPTS & EXPERIENCES, THEY GENERATE MORE NEURAL ACTIVITY AND CREATE STRONGER MEMORIES. INVOLVE LEARNERS IN CREATING MIND MAPS, FLOW CHARTS, 3D MODELS OR SCULPTURES TO ILLUSTRATE THE DIFFERENT PARTS OF A SITUATION AND THE CONNECTIONS BETWEEN THEM. USE ART OR CRAFT MATERIALS, HUMAN BODIES, TOY MODELLING SETS, BALLS OF WOOL, OR RANDOM OBJECTS TO REPRESENT THE DIFFERENT ELEMENTS.

SHOW RELATIONSHIPS AND CONNECTIONS

THESE ARE DEVICES WHERE WE REPRESENT AN IDEA OR PROCESS BY USING A DIFFERENT, MORE CONCRETE OR PHYSICAL CONCEPT, USUALLY TO MAKE IT EASIER TO UNDERSTAND, TO EXPLORE ITS MEANING, OR TO MAKE IT MEMORABLE. WHEN WE USE THESE DEVICES, OUR BRAIN PROCESSES THE REPRESENTATION AS IF IT WERE THE REAL THING, WHICH STRENGTHENS THE LEARNING.

I AM GOING TO...

USE LANGUAGE TO SUPPORT INTENTION

WHEN WE SAY WE ARE GOING TO DO SOMETHING, NEURAL PATHWAYS ARE FORMED WHICH SUPPORT THAT INTENTION AND WE ARE THEN MORE LIKELY TO ACTUALLY DO IT. CREATE OPPORTUNITIES FOR LEARNERS TO MAKE POSITIVE AFFIRMATIONS ABOUT WHAT THEY HAVE LEARNT AND WHAT THEY WILL DO.

USE MINDFULNESS ACTIVITIES & MEDITATION

THESE CHANGE THE BRAIN BY ENHANCING THE AREAS ASSOCIATED WITH LEARNING + MEMORY; EMOTIONAL REGULATION + SELF AWARENESS; AND REDUCE ANXIETY + STRESS.

PROMOTE UNCONSCIOUS PROCESSING

THE UNCONSCIOUS MIND PROCESSES AND ORGANISES INFORMATION AND MAKES CONNECTIONS BETWEEN EXPERIENCES AND CONCEPTS. CREATE OPPORTUNITIES FOR LEARNERS' UNCONSCIOUS MINDS TO PLAY WITH WHAT THEY HAVE LEARNT BY ASKING THEM TO WALK AWAY AND DO ANOTHER TASK FOR AT LEAST 15 MINS AFTER THE LEARNING ACTIVITY

USE ANCHORS

AN ANCHOR IS AN EXTERNAL CUE OR STIMULUS, SUCH AS A COLOUR, SOUND, OR IMAGE WHICH IS ASSOCIATED WITH A CONCEPT, EXPERIENCE OR EMOTIONAL STATE. BY ASSOCIATING ANCHORS WITH LEARNING POINTS, WE HELP LEARNERS TO CREATE STRONGER MEMORIES WHICH THEY CAN RETREIVE MORE EASILY WHEN THE ANCHOR IS PRESENT

MIND

USE VISUALISATION

THE BRAIN CAN'T TELL THE DIFFERENCE BETWEEN SOMETHING REAL OR IMAGINED, SO BY USING VISUALISATIONS TO HELP LEARNERS TO MENTALLY REHEARSE THEIR NEW HABITS, WE STRENGTHEN THEIR ABILITY TO DO IT IN REAL LIFE.

part three

HEART

HEART

HOW TO CREATE EMOTIONAL EXPERIENCES

EMOTIONS INVOLVE THE HEART + BRAIN WORKING TOGETHER. THE HEART COMMUNICATES DIRECTLY WITH THE LIMBIC SYSTEM OR "EMOTIONAL BRAIN" - THE PART OF THE BRAIN THAT DEALS WITH BOTH EMOTIONS AND MEMORY. THE HEART ACTUALLY SENDS MORE SIGNALS TO THE BRAIN THAN THE BRAIN SENDS TO THE HEART, AND THESE HEART SIGNALS HAVE A POWERFUL EFFECT ON THE WAY THE BRAIN PROCESSES EMOTIONS AS WELL AS COGNITIVE FUNCTIONS SUCH AS ATTENTION, PERCEPTION, MEMORY AND PROBLEM-SOLVING.

HEART

NEUROSCIENTIFIC RESEARCH SHOWS THAT EMOTIONS ARE ESSENTIAL TO LEARNING - THEY HELP LEARNERS TO PERCEIVE AN EXPERIENCE OR INFORMATION AS MEANINGFUL SO THAT THE BRAIN FOCUSES ON IT, ORGANISES IT, AND REMEMBERS IT. POSITIVE EMOTIONS PROFOUNDLY AFFECT HOW WE PERCEIVE, THINK, FEEL AND PERFORM, AND THEY HELP LEARNERS TO FORM STRONG MEMORIES WHICH THEY CAN RETRIEVE EASILY IN ORDER TO PUT THEIR LEARNING INTO PRACTICE.

WHEN WE EXPERIENCE A POSITIVE EMOTIONAL STATE SUCH AS EXCITEMENT, JOY OR PLEASURE, THE NEURAL SIGNALS FROM THE HEART TO THE BRAIN INCREASE OUR ABILITY TO THINK, REMEMBER, LEARN, REASON, AND MAKE EFFECTIVE DECISIONS. CONVERSELY, WHEN WE EXPERIENCE STRESS OR NEGATIVE EMOTIONS SUCH AS ANGER, FEAR OR GUILT, OUR HEART SIGNALS REINFORCE THESE NEGATIVE EMOTIONS, INHIBIT OUR COGNITIVE FUNCTIONING, AND ACT AS A BARRIER TO LEARNING.

AS TRAINERS WE NEED TO CREATE LEARNING EXPERIENCES THAT ENGAGE THE HEART AND THE LIMBIC SYSTEM TO GENERATE EMOTIONS SUCH AS PASSION, EXCITEMENT, CURIOSITY, AND WONDER. HERE ARE SOME THINGS TO TRY...

ENCOURAGE EMOTIONS

HELP LEARNERS UNDERSTAND THAT EMOTIONS HELP LEARNING, AND THAT IT'S GOOD TO FEEL & EXPRESS EMOTIONS DURING TRAINING

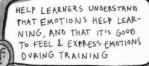

FIND OUT WHAT LEARNERS ALREADY KNOW OR CAN ALREADY DO AND ADAPT TRAINING TO THIS, EVEN IF IT MEANS CHANGING YOUR PLANS.

HELP LEARNERS FEEL VALUED AND RESPECTED - REALLY PAY ATTENTION TO WHAT THEY SAY, WARMLY AND GENUINELY ACKNOWLEDGE THEIR CONTRIBUTIONS

USE LANGUAGE THAT CONNECTS PEOPLE WITH EMOTIONS SUCH AS "HOW DO YOU FEEL?" RATHER THAN "WHAT DO YOU THINK?"

THANKS FOR SHARING

HELP PEOPLE FEEL GOOD

CREATE ACTIVITIES WHERE LEARNERS IDENTIFY + EXPLORE EMOTIONS, AND CREATE SAFE SPACES FOR THEM TO EXPERIENCE + SHARE THESE.

BE AN EMOTIONAL ROLE MODEL - SHOW YOUR OWN EMOTIONS SUCH AS WONDER, EXCITEMENT, CURIOSITY AND TALK ABOUT HOW YOU FEEL

SHOW LEARNERS YOU ARE INTERESTED IN THEM AS INDIVIDUALS - BUILD RAPPORT, FIND COMMON GROUND AND BE GENUINELY INTERESTED IN THEIR VIEWS AND EXPERIENCES

USE STORIES TO AROUSE EMOTION

YESTERDAY I WENT FOR A WALK AND...

ASK LEARNERS TO WRITE/ TELL THEIR OWN STORIES

HEART

USE IMAGES OF FACIAL EXPRESSIONS AND PHYSICAL GESTURES TO AROUSE STRONG EMOTIONAL REACTIONS

MY FRIEND GOT MAROONED ON AN ISLAND...

TELL STORIES AND ANECDOTES FROM YOUR OWN EXPERIENCE TO ILLUSTRATE KEY POINTS

TELL STORIES ABOUT REAL PEOPLE AND THEIR EXPERIENCES

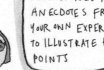

HARNESS THE POWER OF IMAGE

SUBSCRIBE TO A STOCK IMAGE WEBSITE AND TAKE TIME TO BROWSE AND SELECT THE MOST POWERFUL IMAGERY

ASK LEARNERS TO WRITE A STORY TO ILLUSTRATE WHAT THEY HAVE LEARNT

USE MYTHS, LEGENDS AND TRADITIONAL STORIES WHICH ACT AS METAPHORS FOR THE LEARNING POINTS

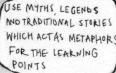

USE CAREFULLY CHOSEN IMAGES TO GENERATE A PHYSICAL RESPONSE IN THE BODY AND TRIGGER THE EMOTIONAL BRAIN

CONNECT PEOPLE TO NATURE

WHEN PEOPLE ARE CONNECTED TO NATURE THEY EXPERIENCE POSITIVE EMOTIONS
SEE CHAPTER 4.2 HOW TO USE NATURE TO HELP PEOPLE LEARN

BEING PLAYFUL AND HAVING FUN CREATES POSITIVE EMOTIONS SEE CHAPTER 4.1 HOW TO PROMOTE PLAYFULNESS

HEART

PROMOTE PLAYFULNESS

FACILITATE AND EMPOWER LEARNERS TO DISCOVER IDEAS, SKILLS OR INFORMATION FOR THEMSELVES RATHER THAN FROM YOU IMPARTING IT TO THEM

CREATE AWE AND WONDER

CREATE ACTIVITIES OR ASK QUESTIONS THAT REALLY STRETCH AND CHALLENGE THEM SO THAT THEY ARE EXCITED WHEN THEY SUCCEED

WHEN PEOPLE BUILD RELATIONSHIPS, COLLABORATE ON TASKS, AND GIVE EACH OTHER SUPPORT + FEEDBACK, THEY EXPERIENCE STRONG POSITIVE EMOTIONS SEE CHAPTER 3.2 HOW TO CREATE A SUPPORTIVE LEARNING COMMUNITY

GENERATE SURPRISE THROUGH PUZZLES WHERE THE SOLUTION IS COMPLETELY DIFFERENT TO WHAT WOULD BE EXPECTED OR TASKS WHERE ACTIONS LEAD TO AN UNEXPECTED RESULT

USE VISUALISATION - ASK PEOPLE TO CLOSE THEIR EYES AND VISUALISE A SITUATION WHERE THEY WILL BE USING THEIR NEW-FOUND SKILLS OR KNOWLEDGE OR REMEMBER A TIME WHEN THEY... (RELEVANT TO COURSE TOPIC)

PROMOTE SOCIAL INTERACTION

SIMULATE THE SITUATION IN WHICH THE LEARNERS WILL BE USING THEIR SKILLS AND FOCUS ON HOW IT FEELS FOR THEM TO DO THIS

MAKE IT REAL

HELP LEARNERS RELAX

USE CASE STUDIES AND REAL EXAMPLES FROM LEARNERS OWN EXPERIENCES

BEING RELAXED IS A POSITIVE EMOTIONAL STATE.
SEE CHAPTER 1.1 "HOW TO CREATE A POSITIVE PHYSICAL STATE FOR LEARNING."

ASK LEARNERS TO THINK ABOUT PREVIOUS EXPERIENCES IN RELATION TO THE COURSE TOPIC WHAT HAPPENED AND HOW DID THEY FEEL?

HOW TO CREATE A SUPPORTIVE LEARNING COMMUNITY

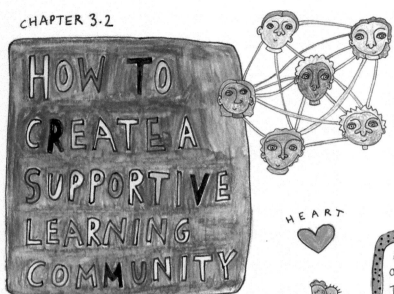

HEART

WE ARE HARDWIRED TO HELP EACH OTHER – THE REWARD CENTRE OF THE BRAIN IS ACTIVATED AND GIVES US MORE PLEASURE WHEN WE DO SOMETHING TO HELP OTHERS THAN WHEN WE DO OR RECEIVE SOMETHING FOR OURSELVES. SOCIAL ENGAGEMENT IS ESSENTIAL FOR BRAIN HEALTH – OUR BRAIN FUNCTION IS IMPROVED WHEN WE HAVE MEANINGFUL INTERACTIONS WITH OTHERS, AND WHEN WE LEARN, WE LEARN BETTER WHEN WE SHARE WHAT WE HAVE LEARNT WITH OTHER PEOPLE.

OUR BRAINS HAVE EVOLVED TO WORK BEST WHEN WE ARE SOCIALLY CONNECTED WITH OTHER PEOPLE.

FOR OUR ANCESTORS, UNDERSTANDING AND CO-OPERATING WITH OTHERS WAS ESSENTIAL TO SURVIVAL, AND OUR BRAIN'S AUTOMATIC DEFAULT SETTING IS TO CONSIDER OTHER PEOPLE'S THOUGHTS, FEELINGS, NEEDS AND GOALS. SOCIAL CONNECTION IS AS ESSENTIAL FOR THE BRAIN AS FOOD, WATER & SHELTER, AND WHEN WE EXPERIENCE SOCIAL PAIN SUCH AS REJECTION, OUR BRAIN REGISTERS IT AS REAL PAIN.

LEARNERS WHO INTERACT MORE WITH EACH OTHER LEARN MORE AND PERFORM BETTER THAN THOSE WHO DON'T INTERACT. WHEN WE COLLABORATE WITH OTHER LEARNERS, WE'RE EXPOSED TO OTHER PEOPLE'S THOUGHT PROCESSES AND ABILITIES WHICH MAKES US THINK MORE DEEPLY AND LATERALLY ABOUT THE TOPIC. WHEN WE LEARN FROM OUR PEERS WE CAN IMAGINE OURSELVES USING THE LEARNING, AND WE IMBUE IT WITH MEANING AND PURPOSE WHICH MAKES US MORE LIKELY TO PUT IT INTO PRACTICE.

WHEN WE FEEL UNDERSTOOD AND CONNECTED TO OTHERS, WE HAVE GREATER FEELINGS OF BELONGING, PURPOSE, SELF-WORTH, CONFIDENCE AND HAPPINESS AND LOWER STRESS, ALL OF WHICH ENABLES US TO LEARN BETTER.

AS FACILITATORS OF LEARNING IT IS THEREFORE ESSENTIAL TO CREATE A LEARNING COMMUNITY WHERE LEARNERS CARE ABOUT EACH OTHER, SHARE WITH EACH OTHER, AND SUPPORT EACH OTHER'S LEARNING. HERE ARE SOME WAYS YOU CAN DO THIS...

SET THE ROOM UP IN A LAYOUT WHICH BRINGS LEARNERS CLOSE TOGETHER AND ENCOURAGES THEM TO TALK TO EACH OTHER

INTRODUCE LEARNERS TO EACH OTHER BEFORE THE TRAINING (BY EMAIL, SOCIAL MEDIA OR BY SETTING UP AN ONLINE CLASSROOM

HELP LEARNERS GET TO KNOW EACH OTHER

As PEOPLE ARRIVE, INTRODUCE THEM TO EACH OTHER AND ENCOURAGE PEOPLE TO TALK TO EACH OTHER AND FIND OUT THINGS THEY HAVE IN COMMON.

MIX UP GROUPS FOR EACH GROUP ACTIVITY SO LEARNERS WORK WITH AND GET TO KNOW MOST OF THE OTHER MEMBERS OF THE GROUP

Hi!

SET SMALL CHALLENGES FOR BREAK AND LUNCH TIMES TO ENCOURAGE PEOPLE TO TALK TO EACH OTHER RATHER THAN CHECKING THEIR PHONES/EMAILS

CREATE ACTIVITIES THAT BUILD RAPPORT BETWEEN LEARNERS BY HELPING THEM FIND COMMON INTERESTS OR HELP THEM TO UNDERSTAND EACH OTHER ON A DEEPER LEVEL.

I LIKE CHOCOLATE

SAME!

USE PEER-TO-PEER LEARNING METHODS

HEART

USE LEARNING METHODS WHICH REQUIRE LEARNERS TO SUPPORT AND CHALLENGE EACH OTHER, LEARN WITH AND FROM EACH OTHER, AND HELP SOLVE EACH OTHER'S PROBLEMS. EXAMPLES INCLUDE PEER LEARNING, ACTION LEARNING SETS AND STUDY CIRCLES (SEE APPENDIX 2 FOR DETAILS.)

LEARNERS CREATE A COLLAGE (PROVIDE MAGAZINES, COLOURED PAPER, PAINTS ETC) TO ILLUSTRATE WHO THEY ARE AND WHAT MAKES THEM SPECIAL AND USE THIS TO INTRODUCE THEMSELVES.

STICK COLOURFUL POSTERS WITH MEANINGFUL QUOTES ABOUT THE COURSE TOPIC ON THE WALLS. LEARNERS CHOOSE ONE THAT HAS RESONANCE AND MEANING FOR THEM THEN INTRODUCE THEMSELVES AND TALK ABOUT WHY THEY CHOSE THE QUOTE AND HOW ITS RELEVANT FOR THEM.

LEARNERS BRING A PICTURE THAT THEY LIKE (FROM A FAMILY PHOTO TO ARTWORK) AND TO INTRODUCE THEMSELVES BY TALKING ABOUT WHY THEY LIKE THE PICTURE. HANG THEM ALL ON THE WALLS TO CREATE A GROUP GALLERY.

WORKING IN PAIRS, LEARNERS ARE TASKED TO GET TO KNOW THEIR PARTNER THEN INTRODUCE THEIR PARTNER TO THE GROUP AND SHARE WHAT THEY HAVE LEARNT ABOUT THEM.

LEARNERS DRAW A ROAD TO REPRESENT THEIR JOURNEY UP TO NOW, USING ROAD SIGNS, BUILDINGS, JUNCTIONS ETC TO REPRESENT DIFFERENT EVENTS OR SITUATIONS, AND TALK THROUGH THEIR JOURNEY WITH THE GROUP.

USE MEANINGFUL ICEBREAKERS

USE ACTIVITIES WHICH ENABLE LEARNERS TO GET TO KNOW EACH OTHER ON A DEEPER, MORE MEANINGFUL LEVEL.

LEARNERS BRING A TREASURE (SOMETHING THAT IS IMPORTANT TO THEM) AND TELL THE STORY OF THEIR TREASURE AND WHY IT IS IMPORTANT TO THEM.

HEART

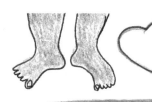

USE SIMPLE TRUST GAMES AND ACTIVITIES

LOOKING AT PHOTOS OF FRIENDS AND FAMILY

WALKING

DANCING WITH A PARTNER

SINGING TOGETHER

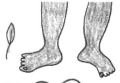

EXPLAIN CLEARLY THAT THE TRAINING OR CLASSROOM IS A PLACE TO TRY THINGS OUT, TAKE RISKS, AND FAIL WITHOUT JUDGMENT, AND THAT ALL LEARNERS NEED TO SUPPORT EACH OTHER IN THIS.

BUILD TRUST

RAISE OXYTOCIN LEVELS - OXYTOCIN (THE "CUDDLE HORMONE") MAKES US FEEL MORE SAFE AND SECURE, SO WE INTERACT MORE WITH OTHERS, AND ARE MORE TRUSTING. TRIGGER OXYTOCIN RELEASE THROUGH ACTIVITIES THAT INVOLVE...

HUGGING OR OTHER WARM PHYSICAL CONTACT

SHARING POWERFUL EMOTIONAL EXPERIENCES (SEE CHAPTER 3.1 HOW TO CREATE EMOTIONAL EXPERIENCES.)

ENABLE THE GROUP TO WORK TOGETHER

ENCOURAGE THE GROUP TO CREATE SHARED, COMMON GOALS FOR THEIR LEARNING OVERALL OR FOR SPECIFIC ACTIVITIES

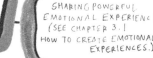

USE STORIES, METAPHORS OR CREATIVE ACTIVITIES TO HELP PEOPLE TALK ABOUT THEMSELVES OR THEIR OWN EXPERIENCES OR PERSPECTIVES MORE COMFORTABLY

H E A R T

CREATE NON-COMPETITIVE TEAM GAMES AND ACTIVITIES THAT REQUIRE GOOD COMMUNICATION AND COLLABORATION TO SUCCEED

USE ACTIVITIES WHICH IDENTIFY DIFFERENT PERSPECTIVES AND HIGHLIGHT THE COMMONALITY IN THE GROUP AS WELL AS THE DIVERSITY.

ASK GROUP MEMBERS TO REVIEW EACH OTHER'S WORK AND PROVIDE CONSTRUCTIVE FEEDBACK USING GEMS (WHAT WORKED WELL) AND OPPORTUNITIES (WHAT COULD BE IMPROVED)

USE THE "1-2-GROUP" PROCESS TO HELP LEARNERS FEEL COMFORTABLE SHARING AND SPEAKING IN THE GROUP

1 - INDIVIDUAL TIME TO CONSIDER RESPONSES

hmm

I FEEL...

2 - SHARING IN PAIRS

I THINK...

GROUP - FEEDING BACK TO WHOLE GROUP

HOW TO FOSTER A LOVE OF LEARNING

HEART

PHILOMATHS ARE PEOPLE WHO LOVE TO LEARN - FOR ITS OWN SAKE AND NOT JUST TO SATISFY EXTERNAL GOALS OR REQUIREMENTS. THEY SEE LIFE AS A CONSTANT LEARNING EXPERIENCE, ARE CURIOUS, HAVE AN INNATE DESIRE TO FIND OUT MORE, AND ARE MOTIVATED TO DEVELOP NEW SKILLS, KNOWLEDGE AND UNDERSTANDING.

IN TODAY'S INCREASINGLY COMPLEX AND FAST CHANGING WORLD, WITH NEW TECHNOLOGIES AND INNOVATIONS CONTINUALLY TRANSFORMING THE WAY WE LIVE AND WORK, THE ABILITY TO LEARN HAS BECOME MORE AND MORE IMPORTANT, AND THE PEOPLE THAT ARE BEST AT LEARNING ARE THOSE WHO ACTUALLY LOVE LEARNING.

THEY ENJOY LEARNING NEW THINGS EVEN WHEN IT'S A CHALLENGE, AND THEY SEE BARRIERS AS ANOTHER OPPORTUNITY TO LEARN BY TRANSFORMING PROBLEMS INTO POSITIVE, ENERGISING EXPERIENCES.

THEY MAKE BETTER LEARNERS BECAUSE THEY EMBRACE LEARNING EXPERIENCES AND LEARN MORE QUICKLY AT A DEEPER LEVEL. THEY ARE ALSO MORE RESILIENT, MORE OPEN TO CHANGE, AND TEND TO LEAD HAPPIER AND MORE FULFILLED LIVES.

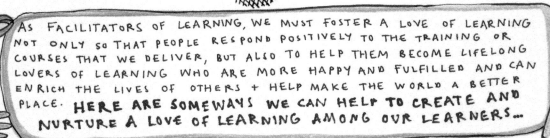

AS FACILITATORS OF LEARNING, WE MUST FOSTER A LOVE OF LEARNING NOT ONLY SO THAT PEOPLE RESPOND POSITIVELY TO THE TRAINING OR COURSES THAT WE DELIVER, BUT ALSO TO HELP THEM BECOME LIFELONG LOVERS OF LEARNING WHO ARE MORE HAPPY AND FULFILLED AND CAN ENRICH THE LIVES OF OTHERS + HELP MAKE THE WORLD A BETTER PLACE. HERE ARE SOMEWAYS WE CAN HELP TO CREATE AND NURTURE A LOVE OF LEARNING AMONG OUR LEARNERS...

ENABLE PEOPLE TO TAKE OWNERSHIP OF THEIR OWN LEARNING

WHEN LEARNERS HAVE CHOICES AND CAN MAKE THEIR OWN DECISIONS ABOUT WHAT AND HOW THEY LEARN, THEY TAKE MORE RESPONSIBILITY FOR IT AND ENJOY IT MORE. DON'T BE RIGID ABOUT HOW YOUR LEARNERS LEARN - GIVE THEM FREEDOM TO LEARN IN THEIR OWN WAY BY LETTING THEM CHOOSE WHAT THEY DO AND HOW THEY DO IT. ENCOURAGE OR ENABLE LEARNERS TO...

SET THEIR OWN PERSONAL LEARNING GOALS EITHER BEFORE OR AT THE BEGINNING OF THE COURSE/CLASS

CHOOSE THEIR OWN PROJECTS TO WORK ON AND THEN SHARE THEIR LEARNING WITH THE GROUP

CHOOSE WHICH IDEAS OR TOPICS TO INVESTIGATE FURTHER THEN PROVIDE THEM WITH LOTS OF ADDITIONAL RESOURCES, INFORMATION AND WEBSITE LINKS.

WEB SITES

CHOOSE WHICH LEARNING ACTIVITIES THEY WANT TO PARTICIPATE IN

DECIDE HOW THEY WILL FEEDBACK/SHARE/PRESENT THEIR IDEAS TO THE REST OF THE GROUP

BOOKS MAGAZINE

DECIDE WHERE THEY DO THEIR LEARNING (EG WHAT ROOM THEY WORK IN, WHETHER TO GO OUTSIDE ETC)

HEART ♥

ASK LEARNERS TO IDENTIFY WHAT THEY WANT TO BE ABLE TO DO OR ACHIEVE AS A RESULT OF THIS LEARNING EXPERIENCE

ASK LEARNERS TO IDENTIFY AND USE REAL LIFE EXAMPLES FROM THEIR OWN WORK/LIFE AS CASE STUDIES OR SCENARIOS

GOAL

FIND OUT THROUGH ICEBREAKERS + INFORMAL DISCUSSIONS WHAT IS IMPORTANT TO LEARNERS AND WHAT THEIR VALUES, GOALS + ASPIRATIONS ARE.

CONNECT LEARNING TO PERSONAL GOALS, VALUES OR PURPOSE

LOVERS OF LEARNING TEND TO CONNECT THEIR LEARNING TO A BIGGER PURPOSE, EITHER PERSONALLY OR PROFESSIONALLY, AND OUR ENERGY FOR LEARNING OFTEN COMES FROM A DESIRE TO DO OR ACHIEVE SOMETHING THAT MATTERS TO US. HELP LEARNERS TO MAKE THIS CONNECTION FOR THEMSELVES AND TO FOCUS ON WHAT'S IN IT FOR THEM SO THAT THEY ARE MOTIVATED TO LEARN.

USE STORIES + EXAMPLES THAT SPECIFICALLY ILLUSTRATE HOW THE TOPIC UNDER CONSIDERATION RELATES TO THE PERSONAL VALUES AND ASPIRATIONS OF LEARNERS

ASK LEARNERS TO CREATE A MAP OR VISUAL IMAGE TO ILLUSTRATE HOW THEY THINK THEIR LEARNING WILL HELP THEM TO GET TO WHERE THEY WANT TO BE.

? ? ? ? ? | ? ? ? ? ? ? ?

ASK QUESTIONS SUCH AS "HOW DOES THIS HELP YOU TO ACHIEVE YOUR GOALS?", "HOW DOES THIS LINK TO YOUR PERSONAL VALUES?" OR "WHAT MEANING DOES THIS HAVE FOR YOU?"

USE LENGTHS OF FABRIC TO COVER TRAINING MATERIALS THEN REVEAL THEM WITH A FLOURISH ("TADA!") AT THE APPROPRIATE TIME.

LEAVE TASTERS AND CLUES AROUND THE ROOM SUCH AS CARDS WITH QUESTIONS, WORDS OR IMAGES ON WHICH RELATE TO THE TOPIC. ASK LEARNERS TO NOTICE THEM & CONSIDER WHAT THEY MIGHT MEAN. WHEN THEIR CONTENT ARISES IN DISCUSSIONS, ASK LEARNERS TO LOCATE AND COLLECT THEM.

CURIOSITY

GIVE EACH LEARNER A CLOSED BOX OR BAG CONTAINING THE MATERIALS THEY NEED FOR THE COURSE OR FOR A SPECIFIC ACTIVITY. ASK THEM TO GUESS WHAT IS IN THE BAG AND HOW THEY THINK THE MATERIALS MIGHT BE USED

PUT COLOURFUL POSTERS ON THE WALLS WITH INSPIRING QUOTES & IMAGES RELATED TO THE TOPIC.

AROUSE CURIOSITY

HEART

ASK LEARNERS "WHAT ARE YOU CURIOUS ABOUT?" AND SHARE IN PAIRS OR SMALL GROUPS

CREATE YOUR OWN CHRISTMAS CRACKERS, FORTUNE COOKIES AND OTHER TREATS WHICH HAVE IDEAS OR ANSWERS HIDDEN INSIDE FOR LEARNERS TO DISCOVER.

CRACKERS

WHEN WE ARE CURIOUS OUR BRAIN RELEASES DOPAMINE, A NEUROTRANSMITTER WHICH GIVES US A FEELING OF PLEASURE AND MOTIVATES US TO WANT TO LEARN MORE, AS WELL AS CREATING STRONGER MEMORIES.

USE PROPS TO ACT AS METAPHORS FOR DIFFERENT IDEAS OR LEARNING POINTS AND ASK LEARNERS WHAT THEY THINK THE PROP REPRESENTS

CREATE A TREASURE HUNT WHERE LEARNERS WORK OUT THE ANSWERS TO CLUES WHICH LEAD THEM TO A "TREASURE" OF KNOWLEDGE

MAKE LIFE A LEARNING SPACE

EMBRACE UNPLANNED ACTIVITIES AND TURN UNINTENTIONAL EXPERIENCES INTO LEARNING OPPORTUNITIES

ENCOURAGE LEARNERS TO EXPLORE A NEW TOPIC AND DISCOVER NEW IDEAS JUST FOR FUN BY SUBSCRIBING TO ONLINE NEWSLETTERS, READING BOOKS, EXPLORING WEBSITES JOINING ONLINE DISCUSSIONS, OR WATCHING VIDEOS

ASK LEARNERS TO OPEN UP THEIR SENSES WALK AROUND QUIETLY AND TAKE TIME TO NOTICE THE SMELLS, SIGHTS, SOUNDS, TASTES AND SENSATIONS THAT THEY DON'T NORMALLY NOTICE, THEN IDENTIFY WHAT THEY CAN LEARN FROM THOSE.

LEARNING OPPORTUNITIES ARE ALL AROUND US CULTIVATE A "LEARNING FOR LEARNING'S SAKE" ATTITUDE WHERE PEOPLE SEEK THE JOY AND ADVENTURE OF LEARNING IN THEIR DAY TO DAY LIVES OUTSIDE THE TRAINING ROOM OR CLASSROOM

HEART

HELP LEARNERS TO MAKE A HABIT OF ASKING THEMSELVES QUESTIONS SUCH AS "WHY DID THIS WORK?" "WHAT DID I LEARN?" OR "HOW COULD I DO THIS DIFFERENTLY?" THROUGHOUT THEIR LIVES

GIVE LEARNERS AN ATTRACTIVE NOTEBOOK AND ASK THEM TO KEEP A LEARNING JOURNAL

CELEBRATE EVERY BIT OF LEARNING THAT TAKES PLACE, WHETHER IT'S ONE OF YOUR LEARNING OBJECTIVES OR NOT

ASK LEARNERS TO IDENTIFY PEOPLE WITH A GROWTH MINDSET (FRIENDS, FAMILY ETC) AND IDENTIFY THE KEY FEATURES THAT THEY DISPLAY.

SHARE RESEARCH FINDINGS THAT SHOW HOW MINDSET AFFECTS ABILITY TO LEARN

HELP LEARNERS UNDERSTAND WHAT A GROWTH MINDSET IS AND HOW IT WILL HELP.

PEOPLE WITH A GROWTH MINDSET BELIEVE THAT THEY CAN IMPROVE THEMSELVES THROUGH LEARNING, WORK AND PRACTICE (UNLIKE THOSE WHO BELIEVE THAT THEY ARE WHAT THEY ARE AND THEIR SKILLS AND ABILITIES CAN'T BE CHANGED OR IMPROVED.)
A GROWTH MINDSET IS ESSENTIAL FOR LIFE-LONG LEARNING. WHEN PEOPLE BELIEVE THEY CAN LEARN AND GROW, THEY DO.

PROMOTE A GROWTH MINDSET

ROLE MODEL YOUR OWN GROWTH MINDSET AND LOVE OF LEARNING. TALK ABOUT HOW YOU LEARN, WHAT YOU LOVE TO LEARN ABOUT, SHOW HOW YOU USE YOUR MISTAKES AND FAILURES AS LEARNING EXPERIENCES

JOURNAL

LEARNING

Part four

SPIRIT

SPIRIT

HOW TO PROMOTE PLAYFULNESS

SPIRIT

WE HUMANS HAVE EVOLVED, LIKE ALMOST ALL OTHER ANIMALS, TO LEARN THROUGH PLAY - NOT JUST AS CHILDREN BUT THROUGHOUT OUR LIVES. OUR CAPACITY TO PLAY, BE PLAYFUL, AND HAVE FUN UNDERPINS OUR ABILITY TO LEARN, WHATEVER OUR AGE, JOB ROLE, OR LEVEL OF EXPERIENCE.

WHEN WE PLAY AND HAVE FUN OUR BRAIN RELEASES DOPAMINE (WHICH MAKES US FEEL GOOD, GIVES US MORE ENERGY, AND IMPROVES OUR MEMORY, ATTENTION AND MOTIVATION), AND ENDORPHINS (WHICH AID LEARNING BY MAKING US HAPPIER AND MORE RELAXED.)

PLAYFULNESS ALSO TRIGGERS THE RELEASE OF BDNF (BRAIN-DERIVED NEUROTROPHIC FACTOR) WHICH IS ESSENTIAL FOR EFFECTIVE BRAIN FUNCTION AND IMPROVES OUR PERCEPTION, REASONING, PROBLEM SOLVING AND MEMORY. A PLAYFUL OR "ENRICHED" ENVIRONMENT HELPS TO DEVELOP OUR CEREBRAL CORTEX (THE PART OF THE BRAIN RESPONSIBLE FOR THINKING, PERCEIVING, PROCESSING AND PROBLEM-SOLVING).

PLAY ENABLES PEOPLE TO...

 LET GO OF INHIBITIONS, BE OUR AUTHENTIC SELF, AND UNDERSTAND OURSELVES AND OTHERS BETTER, MAKING US MORE EMPATHETIC, COMPASSIONATE AND TRUSTING, AND BETTER AT CO-OPERATING AND COLLABORATING.

 EXPLORE POSSIBILITIES AND CHOICES, THINK MORE FLEXIBLY, AND BE MORE ADAPTABLE.

 BE MORE CREATIVE BY STIMULATING OUR CURIOSITY AND IMAGINATION.

 TAKE RISKS, MAKE MISTAKES, AND WORK THROUGH IDEAS AND EMOTIONS IN A SAFE NON-THREATENING SPACE.

 FEEL MORE CONFIDENT BY PROVIDING A LEVEL PLAYING FIELD WHERE EVERYONE HAS SOMETHING VALUABLE TO CONTRIBUTE AND AUTHORITY, EXPERIENCE, AGE OR BACKGROUND ARE IRRELEVANT

AS FACILITATORS OF LEARNING, WE MUST EMBRACE THE POWER OF PLAY AND RECONNECT LEARNERS WITH THEIR OWN SENSE OF PLAYFULNESS
HERE ARE SOME SUGGESTIONS:

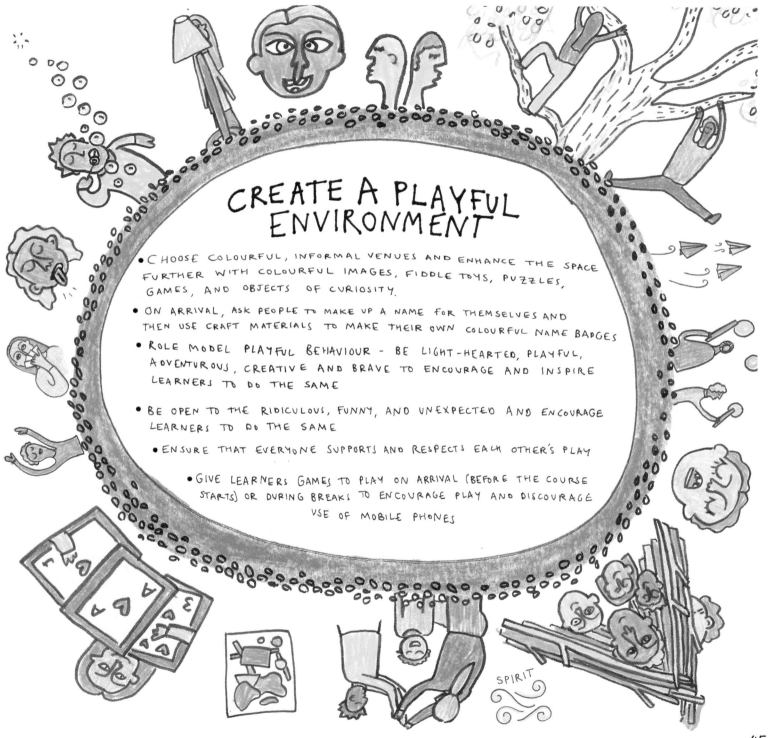

CREATE A PLAYFUL ENVIRONMENT

- CHOOSE COLOURFUL, INFORMAL VENUES AND ENHANCE THE SPACE FURTHER WITH COLOURFUL IMAGES, FIDDLE TOYS, PUZZLES, GAMES, AND OBJECTS OF CURIOSITY.

- ON ARRIVAL, ASK PEOPLE TO MAKE UP A NAME FOR THEMSELVES AND THEN USE CRAFT MATERIALS TO MAKE THEIR OWN COLOURFUL NAME BADGES

- ROLE MODEL PLAYFUL BEHAVIOUR - BE LIGHT-HEARTED, PLAYFUL, ADVENTUROUS, CREATIVE AND BRAVE TO ENCOURAGE AND INSPIRE LEARNERS TO DO THE SAME

- BE OPEN TO THE RIDICULOUS, FUNNY, AND UNEXPECTED AND ENCOURAGE LEARNERS TO DO THE SAME

- ENSURE THAT EVERYONE SUPPORTS AND RESPECTS EACH OTHER'S PLAY

- GIVE LEARNERS GAMES TO PLAY ON ARRIVAL (BEFORE THE COURSE STARTS) OR DURING BREAKS TO ENCOURAGE PLAY AND DISCOURAGE USE OF MOBILE PHONES

SPIRIT

DANCING

PHYSICAL PLAY

STRETCHING

RUNNING

JUMPING

DRAWING

CREATIVE PLAY

SCULPTING

HANDICRAFTS

PAINTING

NATURE SCULPTURES

OUTDOOR PLAY

SPIRIT

TREE CLIMBING

LOOKING FOR CLOUD ANIMALS

TREASURE HUNTS

EXPLORATORY PLAY

NATURE WALKS

HIDE & SEEK

SHELTER BUILDING

ADVENTURE PLAY

RAFT MAKING

ORIENTEERING

BALL GAMES

TEAM PLAY

QUIZZES

TEAM ACTIVITIES

DRAMA GAMES

ROLE PLAY

SIMULATIONS

MURDER MYSTERY

SOLITARY PLAY

PUZZLES

DAYDREAMING

DOODLING

BUILDING WITH BLOCKS

CONSTRUCTION PLAY

CREATING TOWERS

MAKING MODELS

NONSENSICAL PLAY

PURE SILLINESS JUST FOR THE SAKE OF IT!

USE PLAY ACTIVITIES JUST FOR FUN,
OR USE THEM SPECIFICALLY TO ACHIEVE
A LEARNING OBJECTIVE.
A FEW IDEAS:

- MAKING MODELS WITH MODELLING CLAY
- MAKE COLLAGES USING IMAGES CUT FROM MAGAZINES
- BUILDING SANDCASTLES
- MAKING PAPER AEROPLANES
- THROWING BEAN BAGS
- CREATING AND TELLING FAIRY STORIES
- FINGER PAINTING
- MIME
- DRAWING WITH CHALK ON TARMAC
- PLAYING CARD GAMES WITH GIANT PLAYING CARDS
- CONSTRUCTING MACHINES FROM CARDBOARD BOXES
- CREATING PUPPETS FROM SOCKS OR TOILET ROLL TUBE
- PERFORMING A PUPPET SHOW
- BLOWING BUBBLES
- DRESSING-UP
- PLAYING I-SPY
- PLAYING BOARD GAMES
- CREATING AND PERFORMING A SONG, POEM OR RAP
- BALL GAMES
- JUGGLING
- SCAVENGER HUNTS
- CREATING PICTURES FROM LEAVES
- MASK-MAKING
- MAKING MUSIC WITH FOUND ITEMS
- EGG + SPOON OR THREE-LEGGED RACES

SPIRIT

AND FINALLY - BE PLAYFUL YOURSELF:

- MAKE A POINT OF PLAYING PURPOSELESSLY EVERYDAY
  - ON YOUR OWN OR WITH OTHERS
- ALWAYS KEEP YOUR EYES AND MIND OPEN FOR IDEAS AND MATERIALS TO PLAY WITH
- BUY TOYS AND GAMES THAT CAN BE ADAPTED FOR LEARNING FROM TOY SHOPS, CHARITY SHOPS, AND GIFT SHOPS
- FIND YOUR NEAREST SCRAPSTORE AND STOCK UP WITH RANDOM MATERIALS FOR USE IN CREATIVE ACTIVITIES
- SET UP A PLAY CUPBOARD, TOY BOX OR DRESSING UP BOX AND FILL THEM WITH ITEMS THAT WILL INSPIRE YOU TO CREATE NEW PLAY ACTIVITIES

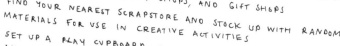

HOW TO USE NATURE TO HELP PEOPLE LEARN

SPIRIT

CONNECTING OUR OWN ESSENTIAL HUMAN NATURE (OUR SPIRIT) WITH THE NATURE AROUND US HELPS US GENERATE DEEP AND POWERFUL LEARNING.

KEY RESEARCH FINDINGS SHOW THAT CONNECTING WITH NATURE CAN LEAD TO:

- IMPROVED COGNITIVE FUNCTION
- INCREASED MEMORY
- MORE INNOVATIVE IDEAS AND ENHANCED CREATIVITY
- MORE POSITIVE OUTLOOK ON LIFE
- BETTER ABILITY TO SOLVE PROBLEMS
- GRETER SENSE OF AUTONOMY + PURPOSE
- INCREASED VITALITY AND ENERGY LEVELS
- INCREASED ABILITY TO COPE WITH CHANGE
- IMPROVED WELL-BEING
- BEING MORE CONSIDERATE & GENEROUS
- A STRONGER SENSE OF MEANINGFUL EXISTENCE
- FEELING MORE COMFORTABLE, RELAXED, SOCIABLE + FRIENDLY
- A GREATER CONNECTION TO OTHERS + THE WORLD AROUND THEM.

NATURE HAS A POWERFUL INFLUENCE ON US. HUMAN BEINGS ARE NATURE AND HAVE EVOLVED ALONGSIDE EVERYTHING ELSE ON OUR PLANET. NATURE IS A PART OF OUR HUMANITY, AND OUR OWN PHYSICAL, MENTAL, EMOTIONAL & SPIRITUAL HEALTH IS INEXTRICABLY CONNECTED WITH THE NATURAL WORLD.

WE HAVE A DEEP-ROOTED AFFILIATION WITH NATURE KNOWN AS BIOPHILIA AND WE HAVE EVOLVED TO FUNCTION BEST IN NATURE RICH SURROUNDINGS

CONNECTING LEARNERS WITH NATURE CLEARLY INCREASES THEIR WILLINGNESS, CAPACITY AND ABILITY TO LEARN. ITS NOT ALWAYS POSSIBLE TO WORK OUTDOORS, BUT WE CAN CONNECT LEARNERS IN OTHER WAYS, HERE ARE SOME WAYS TO DO THIS...

LEARNING IN NATURE

CHOOSE VENUES WITH GARDENS OR ACCESS TO NATURE AND OUTDOOR SPACE

ATTUNE LEARNERS TO THEIR SURROUNDINGS: ASK THEM TO BREATHE GENTLY AND SLOWLY, THEN SILENTLY AND INDIVIDUALLY TO REALLY PAY ATTENTION TO THE SIGHTS, SMELLS, SOUNDS, TASTES, TEXTURES AROUND THEM.

BRING PICNIC BLANKETS AND WORK OUTSIDE IN A LOCAL PARK

ASK LEARNERS TO WALK IN NATURE WHILST DOING INDIVIDUAL REFLECTIVE ACTIVITIES OR PAIRED DISCUSSIONS

OPEN THE WINDOWS SO THAT LEARNERS CAN HEAR THE SOUNDS OF BIRDSONG, THE WIND IN THE TREES

GIVE PEOPLE A SERIES OF PHOTOS OF NATURAL MATERIALS, OR ACTUAL SAMPLES OF NATURAL MATERIALS AND ASK THEM TO USE THESE AS A SOURCE OF INSPIRATION FOR CREATIVE PROBLEM SOLVING

USE RECORDINGS AND/OR PROJECT VIDEOS OF BIRD SONG, RIPPLING STREAMS OR OTHER NATURAL SCENES.

USE VISUALISATIONS WHERE LEARNERS VISUALISE THEMSELVES IN NATURE.

CREATE A QUIZ OR COMPETITION IN WHICH LEARNERS ARE GIVEN A SERIES OF PROBLEMS FOR WHICH THEY MUST RESEARCH EXAMPLES FROM NATURE IN ORDER TO FIND SOLUTIONS.

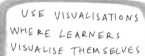

BRING NATURE INTO THE TRAINING ROOM WITH FLOWERS, PLANTS, NATURAL MATERIALS, ESSENTIAL OILS

SPIRIT

ASK LEARNERS TO LOOK FOR EXAMPLES IN NATURE OF THE BEHAVIOUR, MODEL, OR SYSTEM THAT THEY ARE LEARNING ABOUT, EXPLORE HOW THIS WORKS IN NATURE AND DRAW OUT LESSONS OR CONCLUSIONS FROM THIS THAT RELATE TO THEIR OWN LIFE OR WORK

LEARNING FROM NATURE

SPIRIT

EXPLORE DIFFERENT PERSPECTIVES ON AN ISSUE BY CONSIDERING HOW DIFFERENT ANIMALS WOULD APPROACH IT

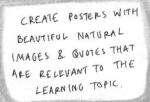

CREATE POSTERS WITH BEAUTIFUL NATURAL IMAGES & QUOTES THAT ARE RELEVANT TO THE LEARNING TOPIC.

USE ITEMS FROM NATURE SUCH AS LEAVES, BRANCHES, FLOWERS, STONES, SEEDS, FEATHERS ETC, AS MATERIALS OR PROPS FOR TRAINING ACTIVITIES

USE EXAMPLES FROM NATURE AS METAPHORS FOR MODELS, TOOLS OR BEHAVIOURS, AND CREATE ACTIVITIES BASED AROUND THE METAPHOR.

LEARNING WITH NATURE

SET UP A NATURE TABLE (WITH FLOWERS, PEBBLES, SEEDS, CRYSTALS, PLANTS, ETC) AND ASK LEARNERS TO CHOOSE AN ITEM THAT REPRESENTS THEM (OR HOW THEY FEEL, OR WHAT THEY WANT TO GET FROM THE COURSE) THEN INTRODUCE THEMSELVES AND SHARE THIS WITH THE REST OF THE GROUP.

ASK LEARNERS TO GO OUTSIDE AND FIND SOMETHING IN NATURE AROUND THEM THAT IS A METAPHOR FOR WHAT THEY HAVE LEARNT

ASK LEARNERS TO CREATE A MANDALA OR SCULPTURE USING THE NATURAL MATERIALS THEY FIND AROUND THEM WHILST CONTEMPLATING A PARTICULAR QUESTION OR CHALLENGE, AND EXPLORE THE IDEAS & FEELINGS THAT ARISE.

GIVE PEOPLE NATURAL MATERIALS (STICKS, TWIGS, LEAVES ETC) TO CREATE MODELS OR PICTURES WHICH ILLUSTRATE THE LEARNING TOPIC INSTEAD OF DRAWING OR WRITING

HOW TO CREATE SPIRITUAL LEARNING

SPIRIT

SPIRITUALITY IS NOT ABOUT FAITH OR RELIGION BUT IS ABOUT FINDING MEANING AND COHERENCE IN LIFE THROUGH:

SELF-AWARENESS - A STRONG SENSE OF SELF AND CONNECTION TO OUR TRUE INNER ESSENCE COMBINED WITH AN UNDERSTANDING OF WHAT WE BELIEVE IN, CARE ABOUT, AND VALUE.

FEELING CONNECTED - UNDERSTANDING THE INHERENT INTERDEPENDENCE OF THE WORLD - THAT EVERYTHING AND EVERYONE IS INTERCONNECTED

HAVING A SENSE OF HIGHER PURPOSE - LOOKING FOR MEANING AND FINDING FULFILMENT THROUGH CONTRIBUTING TO SOMETHING GREATER THAN OURSELVES.

HUMANS ARE SPIRITUAL BEINGS WHO SEEK TO FIND MEANING IN LIFE, AND THIS DEEP HUMAN DESIRE FOR MEANING, PURPOSE, AND CONNECTION IS NECESSARY FOR TRANSFORMATIONAL LEARNING. DEEP, LASTING LEARNING TAKES PLACE WHEN LEARNERS CONNECT THEIR INNER SELF WITH THE OUTSIDE WORLD AND CONNECT THEIR "INNER WORK" WITH THEIR "OUTER WORK".

WHEN WE MAKE LEARNING A MORE SPIRITUAL EXPERIENCE, LEARNERS WILL:

LEARNING AT A SPIRITUAL LEVEL INVOLVES UNDERSTANDING HOW OUR BELIEFS AND VALUES SHAPE OUR BEHAVIOUR, HOW OUR ACTIONS IMPACT ON THE WORLD AROUND US, AND HOW A DEEPER KNOWLEDGE OF OURSELVES AND OUR RELATIONSHIP TO THE WORLD CAN HELP US TO FIND MEANING AND PURPOSE.

CHANGE THE WAY THEY SEE THEMSELVES - DEVELOPING EMPATHY AND COMPASSION FOR THEMSELVES AND OTHERS AND IDENTIFYING THEIR OWN UNIQUE GIFTS, SKILLS AND EXPERIENCES.

UNDERSTAND THE WORLD AND HOW THEY FIT INTO IT - DEVELOPING A DEEPER CONNECTION BETWEEN THEMSELVES AND THE WORLD AROUND THEM.

FIND MEANING IN WHAT THEY ARE LEARNING - EXPLORING THESE LAYERS OF MEANING MORE DEEPLY SO THEY CAN MAKE A DIFFERENCE IN THE WORLD.

HERE ARE SOME SUGGESTIONS FOR ACTIVITIES WHICH ENGAGE LEARNERS ON A MORE SPIRITUAL LEVEL TO CREATE DEEP AND LASTING LEARNING EXPERIENCES.

CREATIVE ACTIVITIES

SPIRIT

GIVE LEARNERS A NOTEBOOK AND ASK THEM TO EITHER WALK OR SIT SOMEWHERE QUIET, AWAY FROM OTHER PEOPLE, ALONE FOR AN EXTENDED PERIOD (AT LEAST ONE HOUR). DURING THIS TIME, ASK THEM TO ALLOW THOUGHTS, IDEAS AND EMOTIONS TO FLOW AND TO NOTICE WHATEVER COMES TO THEM, AND USE THE NOTEBOOKS TO WRITE NOTES OR DRAW PICTURES TO CAPTURE THESE. WHEN THE GROUP RECONVENES, ASK EACH PERSON TO SHARE WHAT THEY HAVE NOTED AND WHAT IT HAS TOLD THEM.

CREATIVE ACTIVITIES HELP US TO DEVELOP OUR IMAGINATION, PROCESS EMOTIONS, AND CREATE A CONNECTION BETWEEN THE SPIRIT AND THE OUTSIDE WORLD. INCORPORATE CREATIVE TASKS OR PROJECTS INTO YOUR LEARNING ACTIVITIES TO HELP LEARNERS TO DROP FULLY INTO THE MOMENT, EXPRESS THEMSELVES, EXPLORE THEIR EMOTIONS, AND COMMUNICATE DEEPER MEANING, FEELINGS, BEHAVIOURS AND OBJECTIVES.

THESE MAY INCLUDE:

- DRAWING + PAINTING
- COLLAGE-MAKING
- USING MODELLING CLAY
- TAKING PHOTOS
- CRAFT ACTIVITIES

SOCIAL CONNECTIONS

WHEN LEARNERS ENGAGE WITH OTHER PEOPLE, ENCOURAGE + SUPPORT EACH OTHER, LEARN FROM EACH OTHER, AND AFFIRM EACH OTHER, THEIR SPIRITUAL DEVELOPMENT IS ENHANCED. SEE CHAPTER 3.2 HOW TO CREATE A SUPPORTIVE LEARNING COMMUNITY.

WHEN LEARNERS LET GO OF THEIR INHIBITIONS AND PLAY, THEY CONNECT WITH THEMSELVES + OTHERS ON A DEEP LEVEL. SEE CHAPTER 4.1 HOW TO PROMOTE PLAYFULNESS

PLAYING

MEDITATION

CONCENTRATION MEDITATION:

ASK LEARNERS TO FOCUS ON A SINGLE POINT, SUCH AS FOLLOWING THEIR BREATH, REPEATING A SINGLE WORD OR MANTRA, STARING AT A CANDLE FLAME, LISTENING TO A REPETITIVE GONG, OR COUNTING BEADS. NOTE THAT EACH TIME THEY NOTICE THEIR MIND WANDERING, SIMPLY REFOCUS AWARENESS ON THE CHOSEN OBJECT OF ATTENTION. RATHER THAN PURSUING RANDOM THOUGHTS, ALLOWING THEM PASS BY.

THERE ARE LOTS OF DIFFERENT TYPES OF MEDITATION PRACTICE. SIMPLE ONES WHICH CAN BE EASILY INCORPORATED INTO TEACHING OR TRAINING INCLUDE:

MINDFULNESS MEDITATION:

ENCOURAGE LEARNERS TO OBSERVE WANDERING THOUGHTS AS THEY DRIFT THROUGH THE MIND, WITHOUT GETTING INVOLVED WITH THE THOUGHTS OR JUDGING THEM, BUT SIMPLY BEING AWARE OF EACH THOUGHT AS IT ARISES.

SPIRIT

WALKING MEDITATION:

ASK LEARNERS TO WALK SLOWLY IN A CIRCLE OR BACK + FORTH, ARMS SWINGING LOOSELY BY THEIR SIDE, OR CLASPED EITHER BEHIND OR IN FRONT OF THEM. WHILST WALKING, FOCUS ON THE BREATH, THEN DIRECT ATTENTION TO THE MOVEMENT OF THEIR FEET, LEGS, THE MOTION OF THE BODY, WHILST OBSERVING THE ACCOMPANYING SENSATIONS. ADVISE THEM TO NOTICE THEIR FEELINGS AND THOUGHTS WITHOUT ANALYSING OR JUDGING THEM AND THEN RETURN THEIR ATTENTION TO THE PRACTICE OF WALKING

PLAY MUSIC TO CREATE A SPECIFIC EMOTIONAL STATE (EG CALM AND RELAXED OR ENERGISED AND ACTIVE)

USE "FOUND SOUND" - ASK LEARNERS TO FIND SOMETHING IN THE ROOM OR THE IMMEDIATE AREA THAT MAKES A SOUND THAT APPEALS TO THEM, THEN WORK TOGETHER IN GROUPS + PERFORM A PIECE OF MUSIC USING THEIR ITEMS

MUSIC

TEACH SIMPLE CHANTS AND FOLK SONGS AND SING THESE TOGETHER AS A GROUP

USE DRUMS, PERCUSSION INSTRUMENTS, OR BOOMWHACKERS TO WORK TOGETHER TO CREATE RHYTHMS + TUNES TOGETHER

MUSIC CONNECTS THE BODY + HEART TO THE SPIRIT, AND ACTIVITIES THAT INVOLVE CREATING OR EXPERIENCING MUSIC TOGETHER PUT PEOPLE ON THE SAME VIBRATIONAL WAVELENGTH SO THAT THEY CONNECT WITH EACH OTHER ON A DEEP LEVEL.

WRITING

This may involve learners writing directly about themselves and their own experiences, or creating stories and metaphors to illustrate concepts and ideas.

REFLECTIVE JOURNALING:

Give learners an attractive, blank-paged notebook, and ask them to record various events that they experience. Encourage them to go back to previous entries at a later date and reflect on them, in order to create meaning from the events, understand themselves better, or identify what they learnt from the experience.

WRITING POETRY:

It doesn't have to be highbrow! Ask learners to write either a limerick or a haiku poem to express an idea or something they have learnt. Encourage them to write their poem on a large piece of paper and decorate or illustrate it then post it on the walls for others to read.

WRITING STORIES:

Ask learners to write a story in the style of a folk tale or fable to illustrate a particular idea, learning point or message, then share this with the group.

SPIRIT

GRATITUDE:
Give learners a jar, box or container of some kind (ideally one they can personalise by decorating it). Ask them to write down things that they are grateful for and put them into the jar. Encourage learners to reflect on these individually, or share with the group.

AFFIRMATIONS:
Ask learners to identify and write down positive statements that reflect their gifts, qualities or skills, or that affirm the fact that they are capable of doing anything that they choose to do. Ask them to write these down and then say them out loud to themselves on a regular basis.

LETTING GO:
Help learners to let go of unhelpful behaviours by writing them on leaves, dropping them in a river, and watching them float away, or by writing on pieces of paper and burning them.

A ritual is a set of actions that has a deep or personally significant meaning. A ritual can act as a metaphor or symbol which helps learners to connect with an aspect of themselves, break old habits, or embrace new ways of seeing or doing things. Use rituals that can easily be incorporated into a training or learning environment

RITUALS

GRATITU

LETTING GO

MANDALAS

Ask learners to create a personal mandala to symbolise their journey through life, to tell a story, or to reveal a path in life, or as a group (provide materials such as paper, pens, paints, fabric collage + natural materials such as leaves)

A mandala is a circular pattern of design which symbolises wholeness, interconnectedness, and the never ending cycle of life. It can represent our inner selves, our body + mind, our families + friends or communities, our teams, our organisations, society, planet + universe. Creating a mandala promotes self-reflection + increases self-awareness.

Give learners pictures of a range of different mandalas (search online for examples) and ask them to choose one which for them represents the topic that is being explored, then spend time quietly looking at it and identifying what thoughts arise.

Ask learners to choose a mandala that appeals to them from a selection of printed mandala pattern outlines (available online). Provide colouring pens or pencils or paints and give them a question to consider while they colour in the mandala (either individually or as a group)

APPENDIX 1

RELAXATION TECHNIQUES

7-11 BREATHING

WHEN THE BREATH LASTS LONGER, THE BODY'S NATURAL RELAXATION MECHANISM IS STIMULATED. ASK LEARNERS TO RELAX AND BREATH GENTLY THROUGH THEIR NOSE, AND WITH THEIR HANDS RESTING ON THE LOWER ABDOMEN, FEEL THE BREATH IN THEIR BELLY - THE ABDOMEN SHOULD MOVE OUT ON THE IN-BREATH AND MOVE IN ON THE OUT-BREATH. ASK THEM TO BREATH IN FOR A COUNT OF SEVEN, AND TO BREATH OUT FOR A COUNT OF ELEVEN

HEART-FOCUSED BREATHING

ASK LEARNERS TO CLOSE THEIR EYES AND BREATH GENTLY. ASK THEM TO FOCUS THEIR ATTENTION ON THEIR HEART AS THEY BREATH, AND TO IMAGINE THEIR BREATH IS FLOWING IN AND OUT OF THE HEART AREA. WHILE DOING SO, VISUALISE THEMSELVES IN A SITUATION WHERE THEY ARE RELAXED AND EXPERIENCING LOVE

NOSE BREATHING

ASK LEARNERS TO SIT OR LIE COMFORTABLY, CLOSE THEIR EYES, AND BREATHE GENTLY THROUGH THEIR NOSE. "FEEL YOURSELF RELAXING AND LET THE STRESSES + STRAINS OF THE DAY FLOAT AWAY FROM YOU LIKE DANDELION SEEDS IN THE BREEZE FOCUS YOUR ATTENTION ON THE SENSATION OF THE AIR MOVING IN + OUT OF YOUR NOSTRILS. NOTICE HOW IT FEELS COOLER AS YOU BREATHE IN AND WARMER AS YOU BREATHE OUT. LET GO OF EVERYTHING ELSE AROUND YOU AND FOCUS ALL YOUR ATTENTION ON THAT SENSATION OF THE COOL AIR ON YOUR NOSTRILS AS YOU IN AND THE WARM AIR AS YOU BREATHE OUT." GIVE PEOPLE A MINUTE OR TWO TO DO THIS QUIETLY THEN INVITE PEOPLE TO BRING THEIR ATTENTION BACK TO THE ROOM AND, IN THEIR OWN TIME, OPEN THEIR EYES.

HAKALAU

USE THIS HAWAIIAN METHOD TO WIDEN LEARNERS' USE OF THE SENSES, CREATE A STATE OF RELAXED ALERTNESS REDUCED STRESS AND ANXIETY, AND INCREASE THEIR ABILITY TO CONCENTRATE, AND TO TAKE IN, PROCESS AND RECALL INFO.

ASK LEARNERS TO FACE STRAIGHT AHEAD AND FIND A SPOT, JUST ABOVE EYE LEVEL, TO LOOK AT. ASK THEM TO FOCUS ON THIS SPOT FOR 5-10 SECONDS AND TO JUST LET THEIR THOUGHTS COME AND GO.

ASK LEARNERS TO LET THEIR VISION SPREAD OUT, EXPANDING THEIR FOCUS TO THE PERIPHARY WHILST KEEPING THEIR EYES STILL, TO THE POINT WHERE THEY BEGIN TO SEE MORE IN THEIR PERIPHERAL VISION THAN IN THE CENTRAL PART OF THEIR VISION.

ENCOURAGE LEARNERS TO LOOSEN THE BACK OF THEIR JAW TO RELAX FURTHER AND LET GO OF ANY SELF-TALK THAT MIGHT BE GOING ON.

ASK LEARNERS TO NOW PAY ATTENTION TO THE PERIPHERAL, WHILE CONTINUING TO EXPAND THEIR AWARENESS, NOTICING ANY MOVEMENT THAT IS GOING ON IN THE PERIPHERY, BECOMING AWARE OF THE SOUNDS AROUND THEM, FEELING PHYSICAL SENSATIONS SUCH AS THE BACK OF THE CHAIR AGAINST THEIR BACK OR THEIR FEET RESTING ON THE FLOOR. ASK LEARNERS TO STRETCH THEIR HANDS OUT TO THE SIDE, WIGGLE THEIR FINGERS + NOTICE THEM MOVING. SEE HOW FAR THEY CAN MOVE THEIR HANDS WHILST STILL BEING ABLE TO SEE THEIR FINGERS NOW ASK LEARNERS TO NOTICE THE RELAXATION IN THEIR BODY + THE STILLNESS IN THEIR MIND AN OPTIMAL STATE FOR LEARNING

PEER TO PEER LEARNING METHODS

PEER LEARNING

DIVIDE LEARNERS INTO SMALL COLLABORATIVE GROUPS AND GIVE THEM AN ASSIGNMENT OR A PROBLEM TO SOLVE. WITHIN THEIR GROUPS, LEARNERS TAKE RESPONSIBILITY FOR COLLECTING, ANALYSING, EVALUATING, INTEGRATING AND APPLYING INFORMATION. ASK GROUP MEMBERS TO SHARE WHAT THEY HAVE DISCOVERED WITH EACH OTHER, AND TO ENGAGE IN A "CONSTRUCTIVE CONVERSATION" WHERE THEY LEARN BY TALKING AND QUESTIONING EACH OTHER'S VIEWS AND REACHING CONSENSUS OR DISSENT.

STUDY CIRCLES

ABOUT TWO WEEKS BEFORE THE COURSE, GIVE LEARNERS A TOPIC TO RESEARCH AND STUDY. PROVIDE LINKS TO RELEVANT ARTICLES OR BOOK CHAPTERS AND ASK THEM TO HIGHLIGHT ANYTHING THAT REALLY STRIKES THEM IN THE TEXT THEY READ, AND TO THINK ABOUT HOW IT RELATES TO WORK OR LIFE, AND TO BE READY TO DISCUSS IT. ASK LEARNERS TO THINK CAREFULLY ABOUT WHAT THEY WANT TO KNOW ABOUT THE TOPIC AND TO BRING EXAMPLES OF BOOKS AND ARTICLES TO SHARE AND DISCUSS WITH OTHERS. DURING THE COURSE, GO THROUGH THE INFORMATION AND GIVE EACH PERSON A CHANCE TO SHARE WHAT THEY FOUND INTERESTING, SPARKING A CONVERSATION. THINK ABOUT HOW TO USE THE LEARNINGS. TIME SHOULD BE LEFT TO DISCUSS WHAT WAS LEARNT OF PARTICULAR VALUE AND HOW THAT COULD BE APPLIED TO THEIR LIVES OR THEIR WORK.

ACTION LEARNING SETS

AN ACTION LEARNING SET IS A GROUP WHICH MEETS TOGETHER REGULARLY TO HELP EACH OTHER SOLVE PROBLEMS, DEAL WITH ISSUES, OR START NEW INITIATIVES. FOR EACH ACTION LEARNING SET MEETING, THE AGENDA SHOULD INCLUDE:

1 SETTING THE FRAME

OUTLINE THE NATURE, BENEFITS AND PROCESS OF ACTION LEARNING SETS

AGREE & CONFIRM GROUND RULES

FACILITATE AN INTRO EXERCISE TO HELP PEOPLE GET TO KNOW EACH OTHER + BUILD TRUST

2 REFLECTIONS/UPDATES

THOSE WHO PRESENTED AT THE PREVIOUS A.L.S UPDATE THE GROUP ON WHAT ACTION THEY HAVE TAKEN SINCE THEN + THE RESULTS OF IT.

3 BIDDING

EACH GROUP MEMBER TELLS THE GROUP WHAT ISSUE OR CHALLENGE THEY WOULD LIKE TO EXPLORE, AND THE GROUP COLLECTIVELY DECIDES WHICH TO INCLUDE (DEPENDENT ON TIME)

4 PRESENTING

ALLOCATE 1 HOUR FOR EACH CHALLENGE.

WORK THROUGH THE FOLLOWING STAGES:

- **PRESENTATION** THE PRESENTER DESCRIBES THE CHALLENGE + HOW THEY WOULD LIKE THE GROUP TO HELP THEM (WITH NO INTERRUPTIONS)
- **CLARIFICATION** THE GROUP CAN ASK OPEN + CLOSED QUESTIONS TO MAKE SURE THEY UNDERSTAND THE ISSUE.
- **OPEN QUESTIONING** THE GROUP ASKS INQUIRING + OPEN QUESTIONS TO HELP THE PRESENTER CLARIFY THEIR THINKING, EXPLORE DIFFERENT PERSPECTIVES AND IDENTIFY SOLUTIONS AND ACTIONS.
- **FEEDBACK** EACH MEMBER OUTLINES KEY POINTS THEY HEARD FROM THE PRESENTER, THEIR RESPONSES TO THIS + THEIR CONCLUSIONS
- **ACTION** THE PRESENTER TELLS THE REST OF THE GROUP WHAT THEY HAVE LEARNT + WHAT ACTION THEY ARE GOING TO TAKE NOW.

5 REVIEW

REVIEW THE KEY LEARNING FROM THE SESSION + ACTIONS TO BE TAKEN. EVALUATE THE SESSION + MAKE SUGGESTIONS FOR IMPROVEMENT.

WHY WE WROTE THIS BOOK

WE ARE NICKI DAVEY AND LAUREN GOODEY
NICKI WROTE THE WORDS AND LAUREN BROUGHT THEM TO LIFE WITH HER ILLUSTRATIONS.

WE CREATED THIS BOOK BECAUSE WE BOTH BELIEVE PASSIONATELY IN THE POWER OF LEARNING TO HELP PEOPLE FIND MEANING, FULFIL THEIR POTENTIAL, AND CREATE A BETTER WORLD. WE ALSO BOTH KNOW THAT HOW WELL PEOPLE LEARN DEPENDS ON THE SKILLS, INSPIRATION, EXPERIENCE AND UNDERSTANDING OF THE TEACHERS, TRAINERS, AND OTHER PEOPLE WHOSE JOB IS TO HELP THEM LEARN. THESE FACILITATORS OF LEARNING ARE PIVOTAL TO THE LEARNING EXPERIENCE AND WE WANTED TO CONTRIBUTE WHAT WE COULD TO THIS COMMUNITY BY SHARING SOME OF OUR OWN BELIEFS, VALUES, KNOWLEDGE AND EXPERIENCE. WE WANT TO HELP OTHERS DESIGN AND DELIVER TRULY INSPIRING AND JOYFUL LEARNING EXPERIENCES WHICH IN TURN MAKES A DIFFERENCE TO LEARNERS, THEIR WORKPLACES, AND THE WORLD AROUND THEM.

SO MANY TRAINING COURSES AND OTHER LEARNING EXPERIENCES INVOLVE SITTING LISTENING TO A TRAINER OR TEACHER TALK, WRITING IN WORKBOOKS, AND LOOKING AT LOTS OF POWERPOINT SLIDES, DESPITE A WEALTH OF EVIDENCE FROM NEUROSCIENCE, PSYCHOLOGY AND OTHER DISCIPLINES TO SHOW THAT THIS DOESN'T WORK. OUR MISSION WITH THIS BOOK WAS TO INSPIRE TRAINERS, TEACHERS AND OTHER EDUCATORS TO CREATE LEARNING EXPERIENCES WHERE LEARNERS DISCOVER WHAT THEY NEED TO LEARN WITHIN THEMSELVES, SHARE FREELY AND LEARN FROM EACH OTHER'S IDEAS AND EXPERIENCES; TO CREATE ENVIRONMENTS THAT RELAX LEARNERS WHILST STIMULATING THEIR CURIOSITY AND CREATIVITY; TO CREATE OPPORTUNITIES FOR LEARNERS TO EXPERIMENT, TO USE ALL THEIR SENSES, AND TO SOLVE PROBLEMS TOGETHER; AND TO HELP LEARNERS TO FIND MEANING AND PURPOSE IN THEIR LEARNING. IN SHORT, WHERE LEARNERS ARE ENGAGED ON A PHYSICAL, INTELLECTUAL, EMOTIONAL AND SPIRITUAL LEVEL.

OUR INTENTION WITH THIS BOOK IS TO INFORM AND INSPIRE OUR COLLEAGUES IN THE WORLD OF LEARNING, DEVELOPMENT, TEACHING AND TRAINING.

WE HOPE TO HAVE PROVIDED YOU WITH PRACTICAL TOOLS AND ACTIVITIES (BODY), INFORMATION AND IDEAS (MIND), A CONNECTION WITH OTHER LEARNING FACILITATORS (HEART), AND THE INSPIRATION TO BE MORE CREATIVE IN YOUR WORK (SPIRIT).

BY DOING SO WE AIM TO CREATE A RIPPLE EFFECT, GENERATING A CULTURE WHERE BOTH LEARNING AND THE FACILITATION OF LEARNING ARE A JOYFUL ADVENTURE AND A POWERFUL FORCE FOR GOOD. WE HOPE YOU'LL JOIN US ON THIS RIDE AND LOOK FORWARD TO SHARING THE JOURNEY WITH YOU.

WARMEST WISHES
NICKI DAVEY & LAUREN GOODEY

WHO WE ARE

NICKI DAVEY

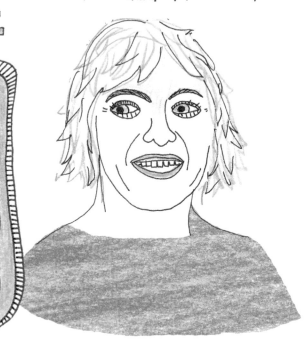

NICKI STARTED HER CAREER IN TRAINING BY TEACHING LIFE SKILLS TO PEOPLE COMING OUT OF INSTITUTIONS SUCH AS PRISON AND PSYCHIATRIC HOSPITAL AND DISCOVERED SHE HAD A FLAIR FOR HELPING PEOPLE TO LEARN, DEVELOP AND GROW. OVER 25 YEARS LATER, SHE DESIGNS AND DELIVERS LEADERSHIP, MANAGEMENT, AND INTERPERSONAL AND COMMUNICATION SKILLS TO COMPANIES ACROSS THE UK AND BEYOND. NICKI BELIEVES THAT WE ALL PERFORM BEST WHEN OUR MIND IS FREE, OUR BODY RELAXED, AND OUR CREATIVE POTENTIAL UNLOCKED. SHE DRAWS INSPIRATION FROM NATURE, THE CREATIVE ARTS, AND HOLISTIC/SPIRITUAL PRACTICES TO CREATE POWERFUL, MEMORABLE, TRANSFORMATIVE LEARNING EXPERIENCES, AND USES FINDINGS FROM NEUROSCIENCE AND PSYCHOLOGY TO GENERATE FASTER, DEEPER, MORE MEMORABLE LEARNING WHICH LEARNERS PUT INTO PRACTICE.

LAUREN GOODEY

LAUREN IS A SELF TAUGHT ARTIST WHO PRACTISES ILLUSTRATION, VISUAL ART AND PHOTOGRAPHY. SHE IS ALSO A FACILITATOR, ORGANISER AND SOCIAL ENTREPRENEUR WITH A PASSION FOR AND STRONG PRACTICE IN SPIRITUALITY, CREATIVITY AND THE NATURAL WORLD, WHICH SHE WEAVES TOGETHER IN HER WORK.

SOURCES AND REFERENCES

BOOKS

- NEUROSCIENCE FOR LEARNING & DEVELOPMENT — STELLA COLLINS (KOGAN PAGE)
- HOW THE BRAIN LEARNS — DAVID A SOUSA (CORWIN)
- THE LEARNING BRAIN — ERIC JENSEN (TURNING POINT)
- A HISTORY OF THE SENSES — DIANE ACKERMAN (VINTAGE)
- THIS IS YOUR BRAIN ON MUSIC — DANIEL LEVITIN (ATLANTIC BOOKS)
- THE BIOLOGICAL MIND: HOW BRAIN, BODY AND ENVIRONMENT COLLABORATE TO MAKE US WHO WE ARE — ALAN JASANOFF (BASIC BOOKS)
- MANUAL OF LEARNING STYLES — HONEY & MUMFORD
- MINDSET: THE NEW PSYCHOLOGY OF SUCCESS — CAROL DWECK (RANDOM HOUSE)
- PLAY: HOW IT SHAPES THE BRAIN, OPENS THE IMAGINATION, AND INVIGORATES THE SOUL — STUART L BROWN (AVERY)
- YOUR BRAIN ON NATURE: THE SCIENCE OF NATURE'S INFLUENCE ON YOUR HEALTH, HAPPINESS AND VITALITY — EVA M. SELHUB AND ALAN C. LOGAN (COLLINS)
- FRESH THINKING IN LEARNING & DEVELOPMENT: NEUROSCIENCE AND LEARNING — DR PAUL HOWARD-JONES AND DR JOHN MCGURK (CIPD)

RESEARCH STUDIES

- BRAIN FOODS: THE EFFECT OF NUTRIENTS ON BRAIN FUNCTION — FERNANDO GÓMEZ-PINILLA, 2012
- NEUROPLASTICITY: CHANGES IN GREY MATTER INDUCED BY TRAINING — DRAGANSKI, GASER, BUSCH & SCHUIERER, 2004
- CREATING VISUAL EXPLANATIONS IMPROVES LEARNING — ELIZA BOBEK AND BARBARA TVERSKY, 2016
- BENEFITS OF MULTI-SENSORY LEARNING — LADAN SHAMS AND AARON R SEITZ, 2008
- THE IMPACT OF PHYSICAL MOVEMENT ON ACADEMIC LEARNING — KRISTY N. FORD 2016
- OXYTOCIN IS ASSOCIATED WITH HUMAN TRUSTWORTHINESS, HORMONES AND BEHAVIOUR — ZAK, P.J., KURZBAN, R., MATZNER, W.T. 2005
- THE EFFECTS OF ACUTE PHYSICAL EXERCISE ON MEMORY, PERIPHERAL BDNF, AND CORTISOL IN YOUNG ADULTS, — KIRSTEN HÖTTING ET AL 2016
- CONCRETE PROCESSING OF ACTION METAPHORS: EVIDENCE FROM ERP — VICKY T. LAI, OLIVIA HOWERTON, AND RUTIV H. DESAI 2019
- FROM MENTAL POWER TO MUSCLE POWER — GAINING STRENGTH BY USING THE MIND — RANGANATHAN ET AL 2004
- EMOTIONAL RESCUE: THE HEART-BRAIN CONNECTION — MICHAEL MILLER 2019
- THE INFLUENCES OF EMOTION ON LEARNING AND MEMORY — CHAI M. TYNG ET AL 2017
- STORYTELLING IS INTRINSICALLY MENTALISTIC: A FUNCTIONAL MAGNETIC RESONANCE IMAGING STUDY OF NARRATIVE PRODUCTION ACROSS MODALITIES — STEVEN BROWN 2018
- EDUCATION AND THE SOCIAL BRAIN — MATTHEW D. LIEBERMAN 2012
- THE COGNITIVE BENEFITS OF PLAY: EFFECTS ON THE LEARNING BRAIN — GWEN DEWAR 2014
- DO EXPERIENCES WITH NATURE PROMOTE LEARNING? CONVERGING EVIDENCE OF A CAUSE-AND-EFFECT RELATIONSHIP — MING KUO, MICHAEL BARNES, CATHERINE JORDAN 2019
- ENVIRONMENTAL ENRICHMENT AND THE BRAIN — MARIAN DIAMOND ET AL 2002
- TRANSFORMATIVE LEARNING THEORY AND SPIRITUALITY: A WHOLE-PERSON APPROACH — GARY PIERCY 2013
- MINDFULNESS PRACTICE LEADS TO INCREASES IN REGIONAL BRAIN GREY MATTER DENSITY — BK HOLZA 2011
- MEDITATION ADAPTS THE BRAIN TO RESPOND BETTER TO FEEDBACK — NATASHA MEREDITH 2018